Shore *gourmet*

Signature recipes from chefs at the Jersey Shore

Credits

EDITORS
Paul D'Ambrosio
Diana Panigrosso

WRITER
Kelly-Jane Cotter

FRONT AND BACK COVER DESIGNS
Tonya Williams

COVER PHOTO
Steve Legato Photography, courtesy of Nicholas Restaurant

PHOTOGRAPHERS
Peter Ackerman, Bob Bielk, Thomas P. Costello, Mary Frank, Dave May,
Tim McCarthy, Bradley J. Penner, Adena Stevens and Michael J. Treola.

COPY EDITOR
Rich Holl

ASBURY PARK PRESS PRESIDENT AND PUBLISHER
Robert T. Collins

EXECUTIVE EDITOR AND VICE PRESIDENT/NEWS
William C. Hidlay

MANAGING EDITOR
Gary Schoening

VICE PRESIDENT/MARKETING
Joe Cavone

ADVERTISING
Don Phillips
Kathy Kersus

Special thanks to James Chehanske, Michael Lorenca, Rosemary Lloyd, James J. Connolly, John Oswald, Steve Strang
and the advertising staff of the Asbury Park Press.
A product of the Asbury Park Press, a Gannett Co. Inc. newspaper.
Contact us at (732) 922-6000. Mail: Asbury Park Press, 3601 Hwy 66 Box 1550, Neptune, NJ 07754.
Visit us on the Web at www.app.com

Acknowledgements

For gourmet diners, we are proud to say, the Jersey Shore has it all. From the tranquility of the beach to the serenity of the woods, those seeking fine cuisine have many restaurants to choose from in Monmouth and Ocean counties. Shore Gourmet presents to you some of the very best in our area.

We sincerely thank the staff members of the News, Marketing and Sales departments at the Asbury Park Press for their invaluable contributions to this publication.

This book was made possible by the personal efforts of several dedicated staffers, among them Promotion Director Diana Panigrosso, Project Editor Paul D'Ambrosio, Staff Writer Kelly-Jane Cotter and Distribution Manager James Chehanske.

I would also like to thank the News Department's photography staff.

We are pleased to present this collection of recipes to you for your dining pleasure.

Robert T. Collins
Publisher

Introduction

Once upon a time, dinner at the Jersey Shore meant fried seafood or spaghetti and meatballs.

Those humble staples are still readily available—and welcome!—but they've been joined by increasingly sophisticated fare.

People travel more than they did a generation ago, and that has led to a more worldly attitude toward food. Meanwhile, the Jersey Shore's population has become more diverse, and menus reflect that change. Latin, Asian and Mediterranean influences abound—dishes are now speckled with cilantro, doused with wasabi, cooled with yogurt.

Seafood options range from scallops caught off the Jersey Coast to tuna flown in from Vietnam. Tuna is now served rare, by the way, and sushi is everywhere.

Restaurants in Monmouth and Ocean counties have received the kind of attention and acclaim that was once limited to establishments in New York and Philadelphia. These are chef-driven restaurants that raise the bar for all eateries, and raise expectations among customers.

And what better backdrop could you want than the shore? Boardwalks and beach towns now boast multi-star restaurants alongside snack shops. The rivers and bays of the Jersey Shore offer fine-dining destinations all along the banks.

But great food is not restricted to marinas or charming downtown centers. Sometimes, wedged into a strip mall is an undiscovered gem of a restaurant.

To that end, we present to you Shore Gourmet.

It brings the best dishes from the chefs of the Jersey Shore into your kitchen. Consider it a primer on Jersey Shore dining. But don't stop with these recipes. Think of them as a way to pique your interest to visit an intriguing restaurant.

Kelly-Jane Cotter
Shore Gourmet Writer

Contents

Nicholas

Nicholas Harary—chef, sommelier and namesake owner of this acclaimed New American restaurant—caters to foodies.

Therefore, he has set aside space in his kitchen for a snug booth that will seat up to four hungry, curious patrons. The table, accented above by an octopus-like orange chandelier, is available for one seating per night, at $150 per person.

Those who sit there will be served from a special menu and will be able to watch the food being prepared, up close. For foodies, that's like a seat behind home plate.

Nicholas, the restaurant, is spare and modern, with understated lines and colors.

There's a fireplace in the back room, a tiny vase of flowers on every table, and a sense of accomplishment and serenity throughout.

Dinner hours are 5:30 to 10 p.m. Sundays and Tuesdays through Thursdays, and until 11 p.m. on Fridays and Saturdays. Nicholas is closed Mondays.

160 Route 35 South
Middletown, NJ 07701
(732) 345-9977
www.restaurantnicholas.com

Butter-Poached Lobster

Butter-Poached Lobster, Black Truffle & Mascarpone Agnolotti, Melted Leeks & Truffle Butter Sauce for Four

INGREDIENTS

LOBSTER

(4) 1½-pound lobsters

1 quart beurre monte (1 pound of butter slowly melted into 1 cup of heavy cream)

AGNOLOTTI OR RAVIOLI FILLING

4 ounces mascarpone cheese

1 teaspoon black truffle oil

1 teaspoon fresh black truffle, chopped

salt and pepper to taste

PASTA DOUGH

1 egg

6 yolks

2 cups flour

1 teaspoon milk

1 teaspoon olive oil

pinch of salt

MELTED LEEKS

3 large leeks (clean and cut into very thin ribbons to resemble fettuccine)

3 tablespoons whole butter

water as needed

salt and pepper to taste

SAUCE

½ pound whole butter, cut into cubes

⅛ cup chicken glace (chicken stock reduced to a syrup consistency)

1 ounce brown butter (butter that has been heated until it is browned and then refrigerated)

1 tablespoon black truffle oil

LOBSTERS: Poach lobsters in boiling, salted water. Cook only halfway through, about 4 minutes. Remove meat from shell. You can do this step earlier in the day if you refrigerate the poached lobster meat.

When ready to serve, heat the lobsters through in the melted beurre monte, about 5 minutes, in large pan. Make sure that the beurre monte does not get too hot or it will separate.

AGNOLOTTI OR RAVIOLI FILLING: Whip all filling ingredients in a mixing bowl until the mascarpone becomes creamy. Do not overwhip or the mascarpone will separate.

PASTA DOUGH: Make a well in the center of the flour. Put the rest of the pasta ingredients into the well. Pull the flour into the wet ingredients with your fingers. Continue until all ingredients have been well incorporated. Knead dough until it forms a smooth ball, about 10 minutes. Let dough rest for 30 minutes. Roll dough out in a pasta machine to the thinnest setting. Make ravioli or agnolotti by stuffing with mascarpone filling.

The pasta can be made days in advance and frozen until ready to cook. To cook, boil in well-salted water just before needed.

LEEKS: Cook the leeks in butter with a little water over very low heat. Add more water if it evaporates before the leeks are cooked through. The leeks should be bright green and tender. Cooking should take about 20 minutes.

SAUCE: Over a very low flame, heat glace in medium pot. Slowly whip in cubed whole butter. The sauce should begin to thicken as the butter melts. Make sure not to over heat. Off of the flame, whip in brown butter and truffle oil. Season to taste.

Have the sauce finished and reserved before you start heating the lobster in step one. Keep the sauce in a warm spot.

FINISHING: Place melted leeks in the center of the plate. Place the cooked lobster on top of the leeks, alternating the tale and claws. Place five agnolotti or ravioli around the perimeter. Spoon about 1½ ounce sauce over the top of the lobster.

Ashes Cigar Club

It's a place to bring your dad, and a key spot for a boys night out.

It's also a haven for anyone—male or female—who feels shut out by the state's smoke-free regulations for restaurants.

Ashes celebrates the cigar. The restaurant offers club membership for cigar connoisseurs, but is also open to the public for dining, drinking, seeing and being seen. Patrons can smoke cigars, pipes and cigarettes throughout the premises, including the dining room.

Autumnal colors and dark wood create a jovial setting at the bar and in the main dining area.

The menu is hearty, specializing in steaks and seafood.

Live music fills the place on Thursdays, Fridays and Saturdays.

Hours are 11:30 a.m. to 2 a.m. Mondays through Saturdays, and 1 to 10 p.m. Sundays. Happy hours are 4 to 7:30 p.m. Mondays through Fridays and all day Sundays.

33 Broad St.,
Red Bank, NJ 07701
(732) 219-0710
www.ashescigarclub.com

Rib Eye & Potatoes

Char-grilled Rib Eye with Yukon Gold Potatoes Florentine for Four

INGREDIENTS

(2) 16-ounce rib eye steaks

4 large Yukon Gold potatoes

6 garlic cloves, shaved

1 cup extra-virgin olive oil

3 tablespoons fresh rosemary, chopped

3 tablespoons fresh thyme, chopped

3 tablespoons fresh parsley, chopped

½ cup Parmigiano-Reggiano cheese, grated

herb oil

POTATOES: Peel and cut potatoes into ½-inch cubes. Heat olive oil in a large sauté pan and add potatoes. Cook until golden brown. Add shaved garlic, rosemary, thyme and parsley. Place in 350-degree oven and cook potatoes until fork tender, about 5 to 7 minutes. Add more herbs and cheese, season with pepper and salt.

STEAK: Season rib eyes lightly with oil, kosher salt and fresh ground pepper. Place on hot grill and char each side. Place steaks in a 500-degree oven until meat reaches your designed doneness.

FINISHING: Remove from the oven, finish with herb oil and let steaks rest for about 5 minutes. Slice into large pieces and fan out around platter. Add potatoes, garnish and serve.

Avon Pavilion

If you're thinking of taking Mom for brunch on Mother's Day, a morning on the beach cannot be beat. Avon Pavilion is the place to be.

But for heaven's sake, make your reservations now, no matter how many months it is until May. That's how popular Mother's Day weekend is at Avon Pavilion, a word-of-mouth place beloved by the locals.

Avon Pavilion is a seasonal restaurant, stretching summer hours from Mother's Day weekend to the week after Labor Day.

Chef Ken Samuels lives and breathes at Avon Pavilion during that brief, intense season. The restaurant serves breakfast, lunch and dinner daily. That's three completely different menus, three totally different crowds. Plus, there's an ice cream parlor! The scene is "beach casual," and how lovely it is. The open-air restaurant is right on the boardwalk, so the salt air drifts in. Lilies and other flowers are arranged here and there to add color.

The dinner menu is light and summery, with mangoes and other tropical ingredients prominently featured.

Breakfast is served from 7:30 to 11:30 a.m. Mondays through Fridays, and 7:30 to 11:15 a.m. Saturdays and Sundays. Lunch is served daily from noon to 3:30 p.m. and dinner is served daily from 5:30 to 10 p.m.

600 Ocean Ave.
Avon, NJ 07717
(732) 775-1043
www.avonpavilion.com

Shrimp and Scallop Karina

Shrimp and Scallops Sauteed with Fresh Baby Spinach in a Light Scampi Cream Sauce for Four

INGREDIENTS

SAUCE

1 pint heavy cream

2 tablespoons butter

pinch of nutmeg

½ cup water

1 tablespoon cornstarch

¼ cup grated Parmigiano-Reggiano cheese

1 pound semolina linguine, freshly cooked

SEAFOOD

12 jumbo shrimp, 16/20 or better, peeled and deveined

12 jumbo scallops (dry pack or diver for best results)

2 tablespoons olive oil

2 tablespoons chopped garlic

1 tablespoon minced shallots

4 ripe plum tomatoes, small dice

¾ cup chardonnay or favorite white wine

2 cups fresh baby spinach, rough chopped

SAUCE: In a sauce pot, place the heavy cream, butter and nutmeg. Bring to a simmer over medium heat. Dissolve the cornstarch into the water and add to the cream mixture while stirring with wooden spoon. Stir until mixture thickens slightly. Blend the grated cheese into the cream. Remove from heat and set aside.

SEAFOOD: In a large sauté pan, heat the olive oil until it lightly smokes. Carefully place the scallops and shrimp in the oil and then add the garlic, shallots and tomatoes. Sauté ingredients until shrimp and scallops are no longer translucent. Add wine and cook until liquid is reduced by about half. Add the fresh spinach and cream mixture, cook for 3 minutes and remove from heat.

FINISHING: Serve over steaming linguine with a slice of crusty bread.

Café Coloré

Café Coloré is a cozy trattoria where guests are treated to a basket of warm bread as they wait for the kitchen to prepare home-style Italian-American favorites.

The interior of the restaurant mimics an outdoor café. Metal chairs surround café tables in both rooms. Mirrored "windows" with striped awnings hang on the wall; baskets of faux plants hang from the ceiling. Muted tones of green, red and gold evoke a sunny Italian piazza.

Lunch and dinner are served. A children's menu is available. Private parties can be booked.

Lunch hours are noon to 3 p.m. Mondays through Fridays. Dinner is served from 5 to 9 p.m. Mondays, 5 to 10 p.m. Tuesdays through Thursdays; 5 to 11 p.m. Fridays and Saturdays; and 4 to 9 p.m. Sundays.

3333 Route 9 North
Freehold, NJ 07728
(732) 462-2233

Pollo Alla Forestiera

Country Style Chicken for Four

INGREDIENTS

1 roasting chicken, about 3 to 4 pounds, cut into 6 to 8 serving pieces

1 cup all-purpose flour

6 tablespoons extra virgin olive oil

½ cup red wine

1 large Vidalia onion, sliced

1 red bell pepper, seeded and sliced

1 green bell pepper, seeded and sliced

2 pounds sweet Italian sausage, cut into pieces

2 medium Red Bliss potatoes, diced to medium pieces

2 sprigs rosemary

salt and pepper to taste

CHICKEN: Preheat the oven to 375 degrees. Rinse and pat dry the chicken pieces. Dredge in seasoned flour.

Heat the 4 tablespoons of oil in large oven-safe frying pan. Add the chicken and fry over medium heat until golden brown all over. Remove from frying pan and place aside.

Drain off some of the oil. Add sausage, bell peppers, potatoes and onions, seasoned with salt, pepper and one sprig of rosemary. Cook for about 15 minutes.

Return chicken to frying pan and toss with pepper, potato, onion and sausage. Place pan in oven for 20 to 25 minutes until chicken is cooked through.

FINISHING: Place on serving platter drizzled with remaining olive oil and garnish with rosemary sprig.

Cask 591

Wine lovers unite! Cask 591 caters to the by-the-glass crowd with a list of 20 wines, etched on the blackboard in the dining room of this inviting restaurant in downtown Long Branch.

Many more can be had by the bottle, too.

A narrow entranceway takes you past the kitchen and a bar into the main room, dominated by a large chandelier and exposed brick walls. Pillows are tucked into booths, adding a homey touch, while piped-in jazz music hints at the live entertainment offered late in the week.

Dennis Tefuri, owner and sommelier, can be found greeting guests, waiting tables and, of course, suggesting wines.

The menu is eclectic American. Tasting menus and pre-theater menus are available.

Lunch is served Tuesdays through Saturdays, 11:30 a.m. to 3 p.m. Dinner hours are 5 to 10 p.m., Tuesdays through Thursdays; 5 to 11 p.m. Fridays and Saturdays; and 4 to 9 p.m. Sundays.

The lounge is open Thursday – Saturday from 6 p.m. to 2 a.m.

591 Broadway
Long Branch, NJ 07740
(732) 571-8848
www.cask591.com

Veal Porterhouse

Veal Porterhouse over Crispy Proscuitto-Potatoes, Fourme d' Ambert Fondue & Port Wine Syrup for Two

INGREDIENTS

PORTERHOUSE

2 milk-fed veal porterhouse, 16 ounces each

2 teaspoons minced garlic

1 minced small shallot

1 tablespoon light soy sauce

1 tablespoon extra-virgin olive oil

A pinch kosher salt

4 turns of the pepper mill

FONDUE

6 ounces Fourme d' Ambert Blue cheese

1 ounce Parmigiano-Reggiano

2 ounces shredded mozzarella

3 ounces shredded Gruyere

4 ounces sweet white wine (riesling)

6 ounces heavy cream

slurry (corn starch & water) as needed

PORT SYRUP

2 cups ruby Port

1 cup granulated sugar

POTATOES

8 Red Bliss potatoes (par boiled until just tender and then slice)

2 tablespoons coarsely chopped garlic

1 sprig fresh rosemary (picked and minced)

2 ounces chopped proscuitto

1 shallot minced

3 ounces extra-virgin olive oil

fresh cracked black pepper

kosher salt to taste

PORTERHOUSE: Combine garlic, shallots, salt, pepper, extra-virgin olive oil and soy sauce in a medium bowl. Mix well. Rub mixture over veal and refrigerate for 45 minutes. Take the meat out of the refrigerator, wipe the marinade off and cook over hot grill. Allow the meat to cook for 5 to 7 minutes. Rotate meat and cook for another 5 to 7 minutes. Flip the meat and continue the same process to cook for 4 to 5 minutes on each turn until meat is done medium. Set aside keeping warm and allowing the juices to rest.

FONDUE: In a medium sauce pot, over medium heat, add the white wine and heavy cream, and then scald. Whisk in the cheeses until well blended. Thicken with slurry to help stabilize the fondue. The consistency should be thick enough to coat the back of a spoon.

PORT SYRUP: In a small sauce pan, over medium to high heat, bring the Port wine and granulated sugar to a boil then reduce to a simmer. Allow to simmer until reduced by about ⅓ or until thick enough to coat the back of a spoon. Let cool to room temperature.

POTATOES: In a medium cast iron pan over medium to high heat sauté the sliced potatoes, garlic, shallots, rosemary and Proscuitto in the extra-virgin olive oil until golden and crispy. Check seasoning and adjust with kosher salt and cracked black pepper.

FINISHING: Place a three-inch by one-inch moule ring in the center back of the plate against the rim and press the crispy potatoes into the mold, filling the moule to the top.

Remove the moule then shingle the veal porterhouse off the center of the potatoes. Split the fondue between the two plates smothering the veal porterhouses with the fondue and then drizzle the Port wine syrup over the plate. Garnish with a sprig of rosemary.

Christie's Italian Seafood Grill

At night, when most of the stores in the Howell Center Shopping Plaza are closed, Christie's Italian Seafood Grill casts a warm glow through its glass walls. Day or night, Christie's is the main attraction in this shopping center along commercial Route 9. An arrangement of potted trees outside the main entrance dresses up the utilitarian surroundings.

Inside, white linen tablecloths offer a crisp contrast to the inviting tones of terra cotta on the walls. Tables are set close together, the better to check out who ordered what, and which dish smells so good. A back room accommodates larger parties. Seafood is the specialty, prepared in classic Italian-American styles.

Christie's serves lunch and dinner. Take-out items are also available. Hours are 11:30 a.m. to 10 p.m. Mondays through Thursdays; 11:30 a.m. to 11 p.m. Fridays, 4:30 to 11 p.m. Saturdays and noon to 10 p.m. Sundays.

2420 Route 9 South
Howell, NJ 07731
(732) 780-8310
www.christiesrestaurant.us

Chilean Sea Bass

Served in a Roasted Garlic Lemon Sauce for One

INGREDIENTS

14 ounces Chilean sea bass

4 Red Bliss potatoes, cut in halves

1 leek

7 cloves garlic, sliced

2 fresh lemons

2 ounces diced tomatoes

2 ounces diced asparagus

1 ounce shiitake mushrooms

1 ounce rock shrimp

to taste: chives, diced; oregano, salt, Old Bay spice, rosemary

¼ cup chardonnay wine

½ cup clam juice

½ cup chicken stock

shallots, diced

2 ounces butter

olive oil

flour

BASS: Cook fish in preheated 350-degree oven for 25 minutes.

SAUCE: Sauté garlic in olive oil until golden brown. Add shallots and chardonnay and cook to reduce. Squeeze the juice of the lemons into the sauce. Add chicken stock and clam juice. Add salt, Old Bay, oregano, tomatoes, asparagus, chives, mushrooms and rock shrimp.

In a separate pan, cook butter with flour, add more or less depending on desired thickness. When sauce comes to a boil, add butter.

POTATOES: Boil in water then roast in oven with rosemary, garlic and shallots.

LEEKS: Sauté in oil with water until leeks are soft.

FINISHING: Add leeks on plate with potatoes surrounding them. Place fish over leeks and pour sauce over top.

Copper Canyon

Downtown Atlantic Highlands has a chic new landmark in the Blue Bay Inn, a European-style boutique hotel.

Within its cozy walls thrives the festive Copper Canyon restaurant. The horseshoe motif tips you off to the restaurant's Southwestern theme, as does the extensive variety of tequilas at the bar. In fact, Copper Canyon offers tequila tastings, for those with a hankering.

Booths and tables are tucked here and there throughout Copper Canyon's multiple rooms. A semi-circular booth in the bar is especially inviting. The decor is warm and modern, in tones of brown and other earthy hues.

Lunch is served Mondays through Fridays. Dinner is served Mondays through Saturdays. The restaurant is closed Sundays.

Hours are 11:30 a.m. to 10 p.m. Mondays through Thursdays, and until 11 p.m. on Fridays and Saturdays.

Private parties can be booked and catering is available for up to 100 guests.

51 First Ave.
Atlantic Highlands, NJ 07716
(732) 291-8444
www.thecoppercanyon.com

Chile Relleños

Panko Coated Chile Relleños with Goat Cheese and Shiitake Mushrooms for One

INGREDIENTS

1 large poblano chile, roasted and peeled

1 cup cooked black beans

4 ounces goat cheese

2 ounces cream cheese

6 sliced shiitake mushrooms

1 tablespoon each chopped parsley and chives

1 tablespoon olive oil

1 teaspoon white truffle oil

½ cup roasted blanched almonds

flour for coating

½ cup panko bread crumbs

1 egg

oil, for deep frying

kosher salt and black pepper, to taste

CHILE RELLEÑOS: Cut a small slit down the poblano chile and carefully remove the seeds.

Combine goat cheese and cream cheese in a small bowl and add kosher salt and black pepper to taste. Mix well. Add ½ each chives and parsley. Mix. Taste. Add more salt if necessary.

Stuff cheese herb mixture carefully into chile. Be sure to press down at slit and seal as much as possible using cheese as your "glue." Wipe from chile any excess cheese.

Coat stuffed chile first in flour then place into beaten egg. Roll chile in bread crumbs until well coated. Set aside for 5 minutes.

Carefully place chile in 350-degree oil. Cook for 5 to 7 minutes until golden brown.

Alternately, you may fry chile in a fry pan with ½-inch of oil. Cook on all sides until golden brown, then place in 350-degree oven for 10 to 12 minutes.

During the cooking, sauté mushrooms with olive oil in pan. When soft, remove from heat and add truffle oil, salt and pepper.

FINISHING: Place mushroom mixture over heated black beans and top with remaining herbs. Placed cooked chile on top and garnish with roasted almonds. Serve at once.

Crown Palace

Crown Palace hearkens back to the days when going out for Chinese food made for an exotic evening.

Two stone lions greet you at the entrance. Inside, the decor is black and glossy, with flamboyant accents such as the gold dragons on a red-velvet wall and the round fish tank about the size of a Volkswagen Beetle.

Traditional Chinese-American dishes fill the menu. Meals end with a fortune cookie and a moist, warm towel.

Crown Palace serves lunch, dinner and take-out meals. On- and off-premises catering is available.

Hours are 11:30 a.m. to 11 p.m. Mondays through Thursdays; 11:30 a.m. to 12:30 a.m. Fridays and Saturdays; and 11 a.m. to 11 p.m. Sundays.

1283 Route 35
Middletown, NJ 07748
(732) 615-9888

&

8 North Main Street
Marlboro, NJ 07746
(732)780-8882

Mango Chicken

Chicken with Mangoes & Peppers for One

INGREDIENTS

1 pound chicken breast

1 whole fresh large mango

½ cup fresh mango juice

2 teaspoons olive oil

½ onion

½ sweet pepper

½ sweet red pepper

¼ cup carrot

1 scallion

4 teaspoons ketchup

¼ cup red wine

¼ cup fresh garlic

1 teaspoon sugar

¼ teaspoon sesame oil

salt and pepper to taste

MANGO: Cut mango in half and remove the flesh. Save the 2 halves of the mango shell for presentation of the dish.

Cut mango flesh into long shreds and cut the vegetables into 1 ½-inch strips.

CHICKEN: Cut the chicken breast into shreds. Put enough water in wok to cover chicken and bring to boil. Place shredded chicken into water until cooked well. Strain well.

Add the shredded onion, carrots, and green and red peppers to wok. Add 2 teaspoons of olive oil. When oil is lukewarm, add garlic, scallions, red wine, mango juice, ketchup and sugar. Heat on simmer.

FINISHING: Add cooked chicken and vegetables mixed with fresh mango. Top with a few drops of sesame oil.

To serve, place chicken and vegetables into mango shells.

David Burke Fromagerie

Back in 1972, when the Jersey Shore was mainly a spaghetti-and- seafood kind of place, the Fromagerie opened in a quiet Rumson neighborhood.

The restaurant instantly changed the culinary landscape and became the place to go for sophisticated cuisine.

In 2006, the venerable landmark changed hands, passing from founders Markus and Hubert Peter to their protégé, David Burke. Burke was by this time a renowned chef, cookbook author and inventor of food products and techniques such as Pastrami Salmon and Gourmet Pops.

Now known as David Burke Fromagerie, the restaurant still has a comfy, French-countryside look. The Wine Bar room, for example, has white wainscoting on the walls and tapestry-upholstered chairs.

Kevin Haeger is chef de cuisine.

Dinner hours begin at 5 p.m. Tuesdays through Saturdays and at 4 p.m. Sundays. Brunch is offered from 11 a.m. to 3 p.m. Sundays.

Private parties can be booked for up to 70 people.

26 Ridge Road
Rumson, NJ 07760
(732) 842-8088
www.fromagerierestaurant.com

Pastrami Salmon

Pastrami Salmon with Honey-Mustard Vinaigrette for Six

INGREDIENTS

SALMON

1 cup coarse salt

½ cup sugar

2 bunches fresh cilantro

1 bunch fresh flat-leaf parsley, well-washed

½ pound shallots, peeled and chopped

(1) 2- to 2½-pound side salmon, skin and bones removed

½ cup molasses

2 tablespoons cayenne pepper

5 bay leaves

¼ cup paprika

¼ cup ground coriander

¼ cup freshly ground black pepper

¼ cup cracked black pepper

HONEY-MUSTARD VINAIGRETTE

1 cup olive oil

¾ cup extra-virgin olive oil

1 tablespoon mustard oil, or dry mustard

¼ cup tarragon vinegar

¼ cup sherry wine vinegar

2 tablespoons honey

2 tablespoons Dijon mustard

1 teaspoon freshly ground black pepper

coarse salt

SALMON: Place the cilantro, parsley and shallots in the bowl of a food processor with metal blades. Process to a smooth puree.

Combine the salt and sugar in a small mixing bowl. Place the salmon on a platter and generously season both sides of the salmon with the salt-sugar mixture. When well seasoned, coat each side with a generous layer of the puree. Cover the platter with plastic wrap. Place the salmon in the refrigerator and allow it to marinate for 3 days.

When the salmon has cured, combine the molasses, cayenne and bay leaves in a small saucepan over medium heat. Bring to a boil, then lower to a simmer for 1 minute. Remove the mixture from the heat and allow to cool.

Remove the salmon from the refrigerator and, using a spatula, scrape off and discard all of the seasoning from the fish. Using a pastry brush, lightly coat both sides of the salmon with the cooled molasses mixture. Combine the paprika and coriander with the black pepper in a small bowl. Sprinkle the spice mixture on both sides of the fish to lightly coat it.

Place the salmon on a clean platter and cover with plastic wrap. Refrigerate for 24 hours. Pastrami salmon will keep, covered and refrigerated, for 1 week.

VINAIGRETTE: Combine the olive oils and mustard oil in a small mixing bowl. Whisk in the tarragon and sherry wine vinegars. Add the honey mustard, pepper and salt to taste. Whisk vigorously for about 2 minutes, or until the mixture is emulsified.

Remaining vinaigrette may be stored, covered and refrigerated, for up to 1 week.

FINISHING: When you are ready to serve the dish, unwrap it and cut the fish, on the bias, into thin slices. Serve with the honey-mustard vinaigrette.

Doris & Ed's

If any single restaurant represents the culinary renaissance of the Jersey Shore, it is Doris & Ed's. It opened in the '60s as a fried seafood place and, by 1998, had evolved into the first New Jersey-based recipient of the James Beard America's Classics Award.

Jim Filip bought the Highlands restaurant in 1978 and, with executive chef Russell Dare, began transforming the menu with care.

Currently, there are three menus at Doris & Ed's: "The Shore Yesterday," with well-executed seafood classics; "The Shore Today," with New American seafood dishes; and "All The Meat That's Fit To Eat," featuring American-raised Kobe beef and exotic Kurobata pork.

A cheese course has been added, complementing the 315-bottle wine list that routinely earns Wine Spectator's Award of Excellence.

The atmosphere in the century-old building is charming, with a crisp, white color scheme, etched glass and pristine views of Sandy Hook Bay.

From September through June, dinner hours are 5 to 10 p.m. Wednesdays through Fridays, 5 to 11 p.m. Saturdays, and 3 to 10 p.m. Sundays.

In July and August, the restaurant is also open Tuesdays, 5 to 10 p.m. Catering is available.

348 Shore Dr.
Highlands, NJ 07732
(732) 872-1565
www.dorisandeds.com

Crisp Black Sea Bass

Crisp Black Sea Bass with Broccoli Rabe, Chorizo Hash, Clams and Saffron Cream for Four

INGREDIENTS

(4) 8-ounce black sea bass filets (taken from 2-4lb. whole black bass)

4 links chorizo sausage

1 bunch broccoli rabe

(3) 10-ounce Idaho baked potatoes

20 little neck clams

2 shallots

1 quart heavy cream

1 to 2 teaspoons saffron

5 cloves garlic

3 ounces basil

8 ounces canola oil

4 tablespoons sweet butter

salt and pepper to taste

½ cup white wine

chervil for garnish

PREPERATION: Scale and filet bass. Score skin and place paper towel on skin to dry.

Blanch basil in boiling water and chill. Wring dry, place in blender with salt, pepper and 2 ounces canola oil, then blend. Strain mixture through cheesecloth.

CLAMS: Steam clams in white wine and shallots, just until they open. Remove clams and set aside, covered.

SAFFRON CREAM: Add saffron to the still-hot clam broth. Reduce to about one third. Add cream and reduce to proper consistency. Season with salt and pepper, and hold.

CHORIZO HASH: Peel and dice potatoes, blanch for five minutes.

Trim broccoli rabe and blanch for 3 to 4 minutes, chill and then drain dry.

Dice chorizo, slice garlic. Sauté chorizo and garlic to release the oils.

Add potatoes, then broccoli rabe, and season.

BASS: Sauté bass in hot oil, skin side down. Place weight on fish to keep the skin flat. Add whole butter until golden brown and crisp. Flip to finish cooking.

FINISHING: Place hash in ring mold on plate; mirror the plate with sauce.

Place bass down and then a dot of basil oil on the plate at the 2 o'clock position. Place 1 clam down with 4 others facing up.

Split cherry tomato and place in center of the plate. Garnish clams with chervil.

Drew's Bayshore Bistro

Chef Andrew Araneo grew up in Keyport and is proud to own a restaurant in his hometown. Drew's Bayshore Bistro, featuring Gulf Coast and Low Country cuisine, is a block from the bay in the downtown shopping district. The cool, minimalist interior, with pale pink walls and sleek black furniture, belies the warm welcome patrons receive. The kitchen is visible from the lobby, and Chef Drew can be seen at work.

The menu is seasonal. Araneo often tweaks the menu or introduces something new when a fresh new ingredient strikes his fancy.

Dinner hours are 5 to 9 p.m. Sundays, Tuesdays and Wednesdays and 5 to 10 p.m. Thursdays, Fridays and Saturdays. Drew's Bayshore Bistro does not have a liquor license, but will provide set-ups if you bring your own.

58 Broad St.,
Keyport, NJ 07735
(732) 739-9219
www.bayshorebistro.com

Braised Wild Boar

Drew's Bayshore Bistro Ancho Chile and Dried Fig Braised Wild Boar Shanks for Four

INGREDIENTS

6 dried ancho chilies

8 dried figs

4 wild boar shanks (preferably hind shanks about 16 to 18 ounces each)

salt and pepper

1 cup diced onion

½ cup diced carrot

1 tablespoon chopped garlic

2 tablespoons tomato paste

1½ cups dry red wine

6 cups chicken stock

4 sprigs fresh thyme

BOAR SHANKS: Remove stem and seed from dry chilies and cover with hot water for 15 to 20 minutes to rehydrate. When chilies are soft, peel off skin and discard. Cut chilies into strips.

Season shanks heavily on all sides with salt and pepper. Sear shanks in high-sided Dutch oven over medium high heat or until all surfaces are caramelized.

Remove shanks from Dutch oven, drain fat but leave brown bits and roughly 2 tablespoons of fat in pot. Add carrot, celery, onion and garlic to pan. As moisture from vegetables is released, scrape bottom of pan to release all browned bits left from the shanks.

When vegetables begin to caramelize, add chiles, figs and tomato paste. Stir continuously until the mixture begins to stick. Add red wine and thyme sprigs and bring to a simmer until liquid is reduced by half.

Return shanks to pot and add stock so that it reaches near the top—but does not cover—the meat. Bring to a simmer, cover and place pot in 325-degree oven.

Cook for 2 to 2½ hours. Shanks are done when a toothpick inserted into the meat pulls out with no resistance. Let shanks cool in braising liquid overnight.

FINISHING: To finish, remove shanks from liquid. Remove all visible fat from top of pan. If left to chill overnight, you may need to heat the pot to release the shanks.

Place liquid and all vegetables, removing thyme sprigs, in saucepan over medium heat and bring to simmer. Remove any fat that rises to the surface.

Puree vegetables, figs and chilies. Return finished sauce to saucepan and reduce to desired consistency. To reheat shanks, place in pan with finished sauce, cover and place in 325-degree oven, or simmer gently on the stovetop.

Best served over creamy risotto, polenta or mashed potatoes.

Due Amici

A baby grand piano, glossy and white, hints at the good times to be had at Due Amici.

A musician tickles those keys in the main dining room every Friday and Saturday night. On other nights, music can be found in the clinking of glasses at the restaurant's inviting bar.

Due Amici serves Italian-American fare in a dining room warmly appointed with wood-paneled walls and a fireplace.

The restaurant is on Higgins Avenue, a thoroughfare known as the gateway to Brielle, a small town along the Manasquan River.

Due Amici serves dinner from 5 to 10 p.m. Mondays through Thursdays; 5 to 11 p.m. Fridays and Saturdays; and Sundays, 4 to 10 p.m.

Due Amici also can provide on- or off-premises catering.

420 Higgins Ave.
Brielle, NJ 08730
(732) 528-0681

Steak au Poivre

Peppercorn Steak in a Grand Mariner Reduction for One

INGREDIENTS

18-ounce New York strip steak

crushed peppercorns

2 tablespoons olive oil

1½ tablespoons butter

1 tablespoon shallots

4 tablespoons Worcestershire sauce, or to taste

1 ounce Grand Mariner

heavy cream

STEAK: Coat steak with crushed black peppercorn. Heat oil in skillet and sear steak on both sides. Finish steak under oven broiler to your desired temperature.

SAUCE: In a separate sauté pan, brown butter and shallots, add Worcestershire sauce, a touch of heavy cream and the Grand Mariner. Cook down to a thicker consistency and serve over steak.

Mahogany Grille

Downtown Manasquan is unpretentious, but lively.

So the Mahogany Grille complements this beach town's vibe.

The new American restaurant was founded by a trio of friends who previously opened the enormously successful Harvest Moon Brewery Café in New Brunswick.

Mahogany Grille is more upscale, but definitely not stuffy. The menu jazzes up a shrimp cocktail, for example, with Bloody Mary sauce.

Dark wood and crisp linens lend a polished air to the interior of the Mahogany Grille, which is accented by Tiffany-style ceiling lamps.

Hours at the bar are 4 to 11 p.m. daily. Dinner hours are 5 to 10 p.m. Sundays through Wednesdays and 5 to 11 p.m. Thursdays through Saturdays.

142 Main St.
Manasquan, NJ, 08736
(732) 292-1300
www.themahoganygrille.com

Hudson Valley Duck

Peppercorn-seared Hudson Valley Duck with Horseradish and Chive Whipped Potatoes, Shallot Confit and Tomato-Bacon Coulis for Six

INGREDIENTS

DUCK

6 Hudson Valley split duck breasts (available in most supermarkets)

3 tablespoons cracked black pepper

salt

HORSERADISH AND CHIVE POTATOES

3 pounds baby red bliss potatoes, skin on, washed and quartered

1 cup sour cream

½ stick butter

3 tablespoons prepared horseradish (or 2 tablespoons grated fresh)

¼ cup chives, finely chopped

salt and pepper

SHALLOT CONFIT

1½ cups peeled shallots, sliced ¼-inch thick

TOMATO-BACON COULIS

¼ pound bacon, preferably smoked, chopped

1 small onion, chopped

5 vine ripened tomatoes, roasted 20 minutes at 425 degrees

¼ cup cider vinegar

1 tablespoon tomato paste

1 tablespoon light brown sugar

Duck: Heat oven to 450 degrees. Place a large skillet on high heat. Score duck skin with crisscross slices. Rub duck breasts with cracked pepper, sprinkle with salt, and place in skillet, skin side down.

When skin begins to brown and fat begins to render out, turn breasts over to sear meat for 1 minute. Turn back to skin side, add shallots and shake to coat with duck fat. Place skillet in oven for 8 to 10 minutes.

Horseradish and Chive Potatoes: Place potatoes in large pot, cover with water and boil until tender. Drain potatoes and transfer to mixing bowl. Add sour cream, butter, horseradish and chives. Whip with mixer on medium high until smooth. Add salt and pepper to taste.

Tomato-Bacon Coulis: Sauté bacon and onion on low heat for 10 to 15 minutes, or until fat is rendered. Remove bacon and onion with slotted spoon and place in blender, saving the bacon fat. Add cooked tomatoes, vinegar, tomato paste and sugar. Puree until smooth and, while blender is running, add bacon fat in a thin, steady stream. Season with salt and pepper.

Finishing: Transfer cooked duck to a serving plate, spoon shallots over top.

Market In The Middle

There is no shortage of cool restaurants in Asbury Park, the grand old resort town that is currently a magnet for hipsters of all kinds.

Market In The Middle epitomizes what's great about the ongoing revitalization of Asbury Park's downtown.

The restaurant is innovative, offering wine tastings, cooking classes, children's programs and samba and jazz nights. It's also eco-conscious—dishes are prepared using organic ingredients, sustainable crops and Fair Trade products.

Organic wines are featured on the eclectic wine list, and there are plenty of vegetarian options on the menu, which changes daily and features cuisines from almost every continent. And it's accessible, both in price and in attitude. The cheese menu, for example, includes descriptions of each variety.

Market In The Middle actually does have a market in the middle, where you can buy some of the hard-to-find ingredients on the menu.

Marilyn Schlossbach, chef and managing partner, also runs the Labrador Lounge in Normandy Beach.

Market In The Middle serves lunch and dinner daily and also keeps the bar open to the early hours. Hours are 10 a.m. to 10 p.m. Mondays through Thursdays and Sundays, and 10 a.m. to 2 a.m. Fridays and Saturdays.

516 Cookman Ave.
Asbury Park, NJ 07712
(732) 776-8886
www.kitschens.com

Thai Green Curry

A Non-Traditional Version of a Thai Classic for Four

INGREDIENTS

2 tablespoons olive oil

1 piece ginger, chopped fine

2 sprigs kaffir lime with center vein removed

1 small piece galanga, peeled and left whole

4 cloves garlic, chopped

1 stalk lemongrass, sliced in thin circles

2 shallots, sliced thin

2 scallions, sliced thin (one for garnish)

5 sprigs of cilantro, chopped with stem

2 tablespoons Vietnamese fish sauce "Nuc Nam"

¼ cup Moi Pae chile sauce

¼ can green curry paste

½ cup sake or dry riesling

2 cans coconut milk

½ cup water or heavy cream

1 bag medium rice noodles

½ teaspoon palm sugar or sugar in the raw

1 quart container of vegetable of your choice. Suggestions are baby eggplant, carrots, squash, snow peas, sugar snaps - anything that is crunchy.

4 to 6 ounces protein of your choice (optional). Suggestions are tofu, chicken or fish.

edible orchids for garnish

fried Asian onion in jar

CURRY: Heat half of the olive oil in pan and add half of the garlic. Add lemongrass, kaffir lime, galanga, shallot and ginger to sweat, but pull galanga out before serving.

Use ends of lemongrass in sauce while simmering then remove before serving. Add sake or dry riesling and simmer 1 to 2 minutes. Add fish sauce and Moi Pae and stir for 1 to 2 minutes. Add coconut milk and green curry.

Add heavy cream or water and simmer for 20 minutes. In a separate pan or wok heat remaining olive oil. Add garlic until you smell the aroma but do not let it burn. Add vegetables and/or protein. Sauté for a minute then add curry.

NOODLES: In a bowl of water soak noodles for 30 minutes. Bring a pot of water to boil and dunk softened noodles for 1 to 2 minutes until they are al dente.

FINISHING: Remove and strain. Place in bowl and top with curry. Garnish with scallion, flower and fried onion.

Matisse

The neo-classical building on the Belmar boardwalk looks like a postcard image from the Jersey Shore of yesteryear. But the restaurant inside is very much about the contemporary Jersey Shore.

Under the direction of Chef Anthony Wall — who owns the restaurant with his wife, Mary — Matisse offers unpretentious, upscale dining. The emphasis is on seafood, befitting the spectacular setting in the heart of Belmar's beachfront, at 13th Street.

Matisse is spacious and comfortable, with high ceilings and an awesome ocean view at almost every table.

Dinner hours begin at 5:30 p.m. Wednesdays through Saturdays. Brunch is served on Sundays from 10:30 a.m. to 3 p.m.

On- and off-premises catering is available. Weddings are a specialty.

1300 Ocean Ave.
Belmar, NJ 07719
(732) 681-7680
www.matissecatering.com

Grilled Chicken Paillard

Grilled Chicken Paillard with Jicama, Oranges and Spinach tossed with a Citrus Pepperoncini Mojo for Four

INGREDIENTS

CHICKEN

(4) 6- to 8-ounce boneless chicken breasts

1 large Jicama, battonet cut

4 cups spinach or arugula

1 small can mandarin oranges

MOJO

1 cup olive oil

1 cup fresh squeezed lime juice

⅓ cup fresh squeezed lemon juice

¼ cup fine chopped garlic

1 tablespoon ground cumin

4 pieces pepperoncini, seeds removed

salt and pepper, to taste

CHICKEN: Place chicken on cutting board or strong table. Cover with plastic wrap and pound with mallet until the breast is nearly twice the size. Coat all with 1 tablespoon olive oil and place on hot BBQ grill. Sear and rotate chicken to form grill marks, about 3 to 5 minutes per side.

MOJO: Place all ingredients in a blender and blend on high for 2 to 3 minutes. Season with salt and pepper to taste.

SALAD: Peel the jicama. Trim to flatten top and bottom and peel with knife in smooth contouring motions from top to bottom. Slice into ¼-inch by ¼-inch logs, or battonets.

Drain Mandarin oranges. Place spinach or arugula leaves in mixing bowl as well as the jicama sticks and oranges. Add mojo and toss.

FINISHING: Place one chicken breast on each plate and top with one quarter of the tossed salad.

Pour remaining mojo in bowl over each dish. You may top the plate with radish sprouts.

McLoone's Riverside

Panoramic views of the Shrewsbury River, plus some celebrity panache, have made McLoone's Riverside an institution on the Jersey Shore.

Owner Tim McLoone transformed the old Rum Runner restaurant and opened his namesake business on the river's banks in October 1987. On Halloween that year, Bruce Springsteen and the E Street Band played a surprise performance at McLoone's, after rehearsing for the "Tunnel of Love" tour.

Newspaper clippings of Bruce hang on the wall in the entry hall, as do stories and photos of Tim McLoone's adventures as a runner and as leader of the band Holiday Express.

Crisp white linens and cobalt blue water goblets highlight the table settings, which are formal but not stuffy.

McLoone's Riverside is known for fine dining as well as for a piano bar that makes for an elegant hang-out. The Boat House deck is open in season. The restaurant is also renowned for weddings and banquets.

Lunch is served Mondays through Saturdays, beginning at 11:30 a.m., and dinner hours begin at 4 p.m. On Sundays, brunch is served from 10:30 a.m. to 2 p.m., with dinner beginning at 3 p.m.

816 Ocean Ave.
Sea Bright, NJ 07760
(732) 842-2894
www.mcloones.com

Champagne Salmon

Wild Salmon Topped with Crab Meat and Champagne Sauce for One

INGREDIENTS

SALMON

1 pound wild-caught salmon filet

½ pound cleaned colossal lump crab meat

CHAMPAGNE SAUCE

1 clove garlic, crushed

1 large shallot, diced

1 sprig rosemary, whole

6 ounces champagne

6 ounces heavy cream

SALMON: Preheat oven to 375 degrees. Place salmon on an ungreased baking sheet after the skin is removed. Place in oven for 18 minutes or until salmon is golden or when white foam appears in the ripples of the filet.

Top with ½ pound of cleaned colossal lump crab meat. Wait to return to oven.

CHAMPAGNE SAUCE: In a small soup pot combine champagne, garlic, and shallots, then bring to a boil. Add whole rosemary, continue to boil, stirring occasionally. When champagne has reduced to half, add cream then lower to medium heat. Allow to simmer 5 to 7 minutes. Strain all garlic, shallot and rosemary from cream.

FINISHING: Return salmon to oven. Place sauce on stove and bring to a boil while salmon is heating. Once salmon is hot (4 to 5 minutes), top with champagne sauce.

Mister C's Beach Bistro

At Mister C's, the bar is so close to the ocean that the rum, it seems, is at risk of going out with the tide.

Every seat at the marble bar faces the ocean, through a wall of windows that affords a panoramic view.

Mister C's Beach Bistro—a white, low-slung building with blue and white-striped awnings—looks like a beach club from the outside. In the dining room, there is more of a tropical atmosphere, with tall, potted bamboo plants and striped carpeting.

The restaurant serves seafood, steaks, pasta dishes, and other hearty fare. There's also a children's menu. The bar features an extensive wine list as well as martinis and champagne cocktails.

A tiki bar gets you even closer to the beach, while the lounge area has a fireplace for chilly days.

Lunch and dinner are served daily from 11:30 a.m. to 10:30 p.m.

Banquets and catering are available.

Ocean & Allen Avenues
Allenhurst, NJ 07709
(732) 531-3665
www.mistercsbeachbistro.com

Sesame Crusted Tuna

Pan-seared Sesame Crusted Tuna with Baby Bok Choy, Shiitake Mushrooms and Thai Chile Salsa for Four

INGREDIENTS

SALSA

1 red pepper, finely diced

1 green pepper, finely diced

2 Thai chili peppers, finely diced

2 scallions, thinly sliced

1 teaspoon finely chopped garlic

⅛ teaspoon total, white and black sesame seeds

1 tablespoon sesame oil

2 tablespoons soy sauce

1 tablespoon Thai chili oil

¼ teaspoon sirachia hot sauce (available at most Asian food stores)

⅛ teaspoon finely chopped lemongrass

TUNA

4 pieces of yellowfin sushi-grade tuna steaks, 8 to 10 ounces each

1 ounce white sesame seeds

1 ounce black sesame seeds

4 ounces sliced shiitake mushrooms with stems removed

4 pieces baby bok choy, halved lengthwise and blanched

2 tablespoons butter

2 tablespoons olive oil

SALSA: Combine all ingredients and let marinate at room temperature for 1 hour.

TUNA: Heat butter and oil in skillet. Mix black and white sesame seeds and coat tuna on all sides. Sear fish in skillet for 20 seconds on each side (tuna will be rare in center).

Remove tuna from pan. Add mushrooms and heat until soft. Add bok choy and heat thoroughly.

FINISHING: Divide mushrooms on 4 plates with 2 pieces of bok choy each. Place tuna on top and then top tuna with salsa.

Ocean Place Resort & Spa

Location, location, location. Ocean Place Resort & Spa is, first and foremost, a place where you can put your feet in the sand and sigh at the Atlantic Ocean.

The Oceanfront Resort features several ways to dine while taking in the view. The Ocean View Restaurant is the most formal. The Ocean View Lounge, Spa Café and the Ocean View Outdoor Café are more casual. All feature eclectic American fare, heavy on the seafood.

The location became even more noteworthy with the opening of the resort's new neighbor, Pier Village, an upscale center for shopping, dining and condo living.

Dining options at Ocean Place Resort vary by season.

1 Ocean Blvd.
Long Branch, NJ 07740
(800) 411-6493
www.oceanplaceresort.com

Curried Prawns with Okra

A Southern Dish with an Asian Twist for Two

INGREDIENTS

MAIN

12 medium prawns, peeled and deveined

12 okra

3 tablespoons vegetable oil

2 tablespoons lime juice

5 tablespoons water

1 tomato, quartered

1 teaspoon salt

1 teaspoon sugar

2 tablespoons coconut milk

SPICE PASTE

4 dried red chilies

10 shallots, peeled

2 stalks lemongrass, cut to ¼ inch pieces

6 candlenuts

1 teaspoon shrimp paste

¾ teaspoon turmeric, ground

SPICE PASTE: Reconstitute dried chilies in hot water for 5 minutes. Grind spice ingredients into a fine paste, preferably using a mortar and pestle, or a grinder. The paste can be prepared in advance and kept frozen until needed.

OKRA: Trim off okra stems and pointed ends and discard. Cut okra into bite-size pieces and blanch in boiling water for 90 seconds. Drain and rinse in cold water. Heat oil in a wok over medium heat and fry paste until thickened and fragrant, about 3 to 4 minutes.

FINISHING: Add prawns and stir fry for 1 minute. Add okra and remaining ingredients and stir fry for 3 to 4 minutes until prawns are cooked.

Palumbo's

P alumbo's offers a quiet haven, just off the Garden State Parkway, for hungry travelers heading to the Asbury Park area.

The fine Italian restaurant is located in a busy shopping center, but the interior is peaceful and airy. Green marbled columns hint at the glory that was Rome and strings of white lights twinkle on the windows.

The menu reads like a greatest-hits of traditional Italian- American dishes, while the cocktail list gives a nod to the Jersey Shore, with the "Point Pleasant Devil."

A cozy bar and a spacious ballroom complete the picture. Palumbo's serves lunch and dinner in the dining room and caters events for 30 to 400 in its ballroom.

Lunch is served Tuesdays through Fridays from 11:30 a.m. to 3 p.m. Dinner is served Tuesdays through Sundays, 4:30 to 11 p.m. Palumbo's is closed Mondays.

Asbury Avenue and Green Grove Road
Tinton Falls, NJ 07753
(732) 922-6690
www.palumbosbanquets.com

Veal Maximo

Veal served in a Brandy Demi-Glaze for One

INGREDIENTS

(3) 4-ounce pieces thin veal cutlets

4 tablespoons vegetable oil

2 tablespoons olive oil

¼ cup brandy

chopped garlic clove

1 cup mushrooms

½ cup sun-dried tomatoes

½ cup chicken stock

1 cup demi-glace

3 to 4 spears asparagus

3 slices mozzarella cheese

VEAL & SAUCE: Bread veal lightly with flour. Drop in hot vegetable oil, browning both sides of the veal. Add olive oil and chopped garlic. Saute and then drain off oil. Add a pinch of salt and pepper. Add brandy—don't stand too close, as it will flare.

Add sun-dried tomatoes and mushrooms. Add one ladle of chicken stock and a cup of demi-glace. Cover and heat on high for five minutes.

FINISHING: Place contents of pan in oven safe dish. Top with asparagus and three pieces of mozzarella cheese. Bake at 400 degrees for five minutes, or until cheese melts. Garnish with basil and a slice of orange.

Pino's

The larger-than-life mansions of Marlboro have nothing on Pino's, which stands on Route 9 like a gargantuan shrine to fine dining.

The parking lot is huge; the bar is imposing; the brick ovens roar with flame as you first walk in. Pastries are displayed like jewels in a nearby case. The decor is clubby, with dark woods, a navy-and-cream color scheme and a fireplace.

The restaurant specializes in fine Italian-American cuisine and brick-oven pizza.

Pino's serves lunch and dinner. Hours are noon to 10 p.m. Tuesdays through Thursdays; noon to 11 p.m. Fridays and Saturdays; and 1 p.m. to 10 p.m. Sundays.

448 Route 9 North
Marlboro, NJ 07726
(732) 972-6663

Colorado Lamb, Beef & Day Boat Halibut Trio

Two-Bone Colorado Lamb, Kobe Beef, Day Boat Halibut with Three Sauces for One

INGREDIENTS

LAMB, BEEF & FISH

1 twin-bone American rack of lamb

3-ounce filet of halibut

4-ounce Kobe beef strip loin

Coarse salt and cracked black pepper

1 ounce extra virgin olive oil

3 ounces aged balsamic vinegar

1 ounce sherry wine

1 sprig rosemary

4 ounces butter

1 shallot

3 ounces Port

2 ounces white wine

3 garlic cloves, whole

2 basil leaves

1 porcini mushroom

1 plum tomato

KOBE: BALSAMIC REDUCTION

3 ounces aged balsamic vinegar

1 ounce sherry wine

1 sprig fresh rosemary

2 ounces butter

LAMB: PORT WINE REDUCTION

shallot

3 ounces Port

2 ounces butter

HALIBUT: TOMATO PORCINI REDUCTION

garlic cloves

1 ounce olive oil

2 ounces white wine

fresh basil

1 porcini mushroom

1 plum tomato

LAMB, BEEF AND FISH: Salt and pepper both sides of lamb, pan sear in olive oil and put aside. Salt and pepper Kobe beef, hot sear in cast iron skillet and put aside.

Salt and pepper halibut, pan sear and put aside.

LAMB PORT WINE REDUCTION: Roast shallot with 3 ounces of Port wine and 2 ounces of butter.

HALIBUT TOMATO PORCINI REDUCTION: Roast garlic cloves in 1 ounce of olive oil then add 2 ounces of white wine, fresh basil, 1 porcini mushroom and plum tomato. You may either slice the tomato beforehand or break it up during the reduction process.

SAUCES: Using separate pans, reduce each sauce to 1½ tablespoons.

FINISHING: Preheat oven to 450 degrees. Finish lamb, beef and fish in oven to desired temperature. Arrange nicely on plate and drizzle each sauce to its appropriate mate. Garnish with your favorite vegetable.

Raven & the Peach

Softly lit, carpeted and dotted with potted palm trees, the Raven & the Peach radiates tranquility and luxury.

Couches and semi-circular booths keep the atmosphere cozy, while a sleek bar adds a touch of glamour. This fine dining spot mixes elegance with comfort, much as Fair Haven itself does. The Raven & the Peach is located downtown in this quaint, affluent, riverside suburb.

The menu created by chef Matthew Zappoli emphasizes refined American Cuisine.

A banquet room upstairs caters to weddings and parties. The intimate Tea Room is open for lunch.

Lunch is served from 11:30 a.m. to 2:30 p.m. Mondays through Fridays; and dinner is served from 5 to 10 p.m. Mondays through Saturdays, and 5:30 to 10 p.m. Sundays. Private parties are available.

740 River Road
Fair Haven, NJ 07704
(732) 747-4666
www.ravenandthepeach.zoomshare.com

Fennel-Crusted Yellowfin Tuna

Fennel-Crusted Yellowfin Tuna With Basmati Rice Cake and Blood Orange Reduction for Four

INGREDIENTS

BASMATI RICE CAKES

2 cups Basmati rice
3 cups chicken stock
½ cup onion, minced
2 tablespoons butter
1 cup fennel, diced and caramelized
1 tablespoon parsley, chopped

1 tablespoon chives, chopped
1 tablespoon Parmesan, grated
1 cup flour
1 cup eggs
1 cup panko bread crumbs

TUNA

4 7-ounce tuna steaks
2 tablespoons ground fennel seed
4 each Basmati rice cakes
2 cups blood orange juice
1 tablespoon shallots, chopped
1 tablespoon butter
1 cup fennel, shaved
½ cup frisee (curly endive)
1 tablespoon chive oil

4 each firesticks
1 teaspoon chives, chopped
1 teaspoon parsley, chopped
½ teaspoon thyme, chopped
12 each popcorn shoots
1 tablespoon salt
1 teaspoon pepper
2 tablespoon olive oil

BASMATI RICE CAKES: Sweat the onions in the butter. Add the rice and the chicken stock. Bring to a boil, then lower to a simmer. Cover, allow to cook for about 20 minutes or until the rice is cooked and the chicken stock is absorbed. Add the fennel, cheese and herbs.

Cool, then form into 3 ounce cakes. Flour, egg then bread. Refrigerate till ready to use. Do not eat until deep fried as directed below.

TUNA: Season tuna steaks with salt and pepper. Dredge two sides in the ground fennel seeds. Heat half the olive oil in a large skillet. Drop the rice cakes into a deep fryer at 350 degrees. When the oil is hot in the skillet, add the tuna steaks, crust side down.

Turn the steaks when the crust is lightly browned, about 3 minutes. Remove the tuna steaks, add the shallots, blood orange and butter. Reduce till the sauce becomes thick and creamy. Finish with a bit of chopped chives, thyme and parsley. Toss the shaved fennel, add frisee with a touch of olive oil, salt and pepper.

FINISHING: Place the rice cakes in the center of the plate. Top with the fennel and frisee. Slice the tuna and fan around the rice cake. Drizzle the blood orange sauce around the plate, followed by the chive oil.

Garnish with firesticks and popcorn shoots.

Rooney's Oceanfront Restaurant

Rooney's is all about the view—and the food.

The oceanfront restaurant seems to be made of glass and air, the better to take in the waves, the promenade and the Long Branch beach. When the weather is fine, seating extends to a bi-level deck, from which you can practically dig your toes into the sand.

Rooney's specializes in lobster, seafood, pasta and steaks, and is renowned for its wine list, which has been acclaimed multiple times by Wine Spectator magazine.

Rooney's opened in 1995 and, was a destination restaurant long before the current revitalization of the Long Branch beachfront.

Pier Village, the upscale shopping and dining center, is located just south of Rooney's. The restaurant itself is now surrounded by a luxury condo complex, making it a likely hang-out for Long Branch's newest residents.

Lunch and dinner are served daily. Lunch hours are 11:30 a.m. to 4 p.m. Dinner hours are 4 to 10 p.m. Sundays through Thursdays, and 4 to 11 p.m. Fridays and Saturdays.

Sunday brunch hours are 10 a.m. to 2 p.m.

100 Ocean Ave.
Long Branch, NJ 07740
(732) 870-1200
www.rooneysocean.com

Ocean Jack's Florida Grouper

Florida Grouper, Broccoli Rabe & Rock Shrimp for Four

INGREDIENTS

(4) 8-ounce thick fillets of Florida grouper

1 bunch broccoli rabe

3 ounces sun-dried tomatoes

12 ounces rock shrimp

4 ounces olive oil

6 cloves garlic

4 sprigs parsley

4 lemon wedges

PREPERATION: Cut stems off of the broccoli rabe and discard. Wash it thoroughly. Cut sun-dried tomatoes into thin strips. Thinly slice garlic cloves. In a pot of boiling water, blanch the rock shrimp, strain and place into an ice bath.

GROUPER: Preheat grill on medium to high for 5 minutes. Lightly oil and season grouper with salt and pepper then place on grill. Grill flat side for about 8 minutes, depending on thickness, then turn and grill an additional 5 minutes with the cover closed.

While the grouper is cooking, heat olive oil in a large sauté pan on a medium to high flame and add garlic until lightly brown. Add broccoli rabe, sun-dried tomatoes and shrimp. Sauté for about 5 minutes, tossing frequently.

FINISHING: Place ¼ of the sauté in the middle of a plate. Place grouper on top and garnish with a lemon wedge and a sprig of parsley. May be served with roasted red bliss potatoes.

Sallee Tee's

T ucked away in quiet, residential Monmouth Beach, Sallee Tee's bustles with energy. Sallee Tee's is a major favorite with the locals, from the boaters at the adjacent Channel Club Marina to families with little kids. With its prime location on the Shrewsbury River and the subtle use of retro-'50s design elements, Sallee Tee's offers old-school Jersey Shore appeal.

The ambitious menu tells the rest of the story, with seafood and steaks, pasta, New York-style deli sandwiches, old-fashioned desserts and a knock-out pickle bar. There's also a children's menu.

Namesake owner Sal Tringola can be found presiding at Sallee Tee's day and night. An outdoor bar and patio puts you at water's edge. The main dining room also overlooks the river and features a fish tank. The Fagedaboutit Lounge is an inviting place for cocktails. Parties can be booked in the private dining room, which has a fireplace.

Most days, lunch begins around 11 a.m. and slides right into dinner hours, from 4 to 10 p.m. on weekdays and 4 to 11 p.m. weekends. Sunday brunch runs from 11 a.m. to 2 p.m.

33 West St.
Monmouth Beach, NJ 07750
(732) 870-8999
www.salleeteesgrille.com

Diane's Hot and Spicy Shrimp

Spicy Bayou Garlic Shrimp for Two

INGREDIENTS

12 jumbo shrimp, peeled

2 ounces all-purpose flour

4 ounces vegetable or blended oil

1 tablespoon chopped garlic

2 teaspoons Cajun seasoning

1 teaspoon paprika

1 or 2 teaspoons crushed red pepper, depending on taste

4 ounces dry white wine

6 ounces chicken stock

2 tablespoons grated Pecorino Romano cheese

1 tablespoon fresh chopped curly parsley (washed and wrung out)

2 tablespoons beurre manie (2 tablespoons of butter mashed in your hand with about the same amount of flour)

salt and pepper to taste

SHRIMP: Dust shrimp in the flour. Heat oil to just shy of the smoking point. Add shrimp and lightly salt and pepper them. Turn shrimp, add garlic and sauté for about 30 seconds. Add Cajun seasoning, paprika and sauté an additional 1 minute.

Add wine to deglaze the pan. Let cook for about 1 minute, then add chicken stock. Add cheese and parsley. Finish with your beurre manie.

Let cook until butter melts and sauce thickens slightly.

FINISHING: Serve immediately, placing shrimp in small bowl and pouring sauce over top.

Salt Creek Grille

The Salt Creek Grille stands at the banks of the Navesink River, next to the scenic Oceanic Bridge in tiny Rumson.

The restaurant makes the most of its river views. Walls of windows border the main dining room. Craftsman-style architecture creates a streamlined ambience, inside and out.

Inside the main entrance, benches surround a roaring fireplace. It's an inviting spot at which to linger after a meal, or while waiting for a table at this bustling establishment.

Seafood and steaks, prepared on a mesquite grill, dominate the menu.

Dinner hours are 5 to 10 p.m. Sundays through Thursdays and 5 to 11 p.m. Fridays and Saturdays. Cocktails are served from 4 p.m., with happy hours from 4 to 6:30 p.m.

A buffet champagne brunch is served from 11 a.m. to 2:30 p.m. Sundays.

Salt Creek Grille offers dock-and-dine service for boaters wishing to come ashore.

Banquets at Salt Creek can accommodate 20 to more than 150 guests.

Friday nights feature live entertainment by local singers, usually jazz and pop standards.

4 Bingham Ave.,
Rumson, NJ 07760
(732) 933-9272
www.saltcreekgrille.com

Braised Short Ribs

Braised Short Ribs with a Tawny Port Wine Demi-Glace for Four

INGREDIENTS

8 pounds short ribs (bone in)

½ cup olive oil

½ cup peeled garlic cloves

2 quarts chicken broth

1 pound carrots, medium dice

1 bunch celery, medium dice

1 pound onions, medium dice

2 cups flour for dredging

2 quarts tawny Port

salt and black pepper to taste

SHORT RIBS: In a large sauté pan, caramelize the vegetables with the olive oil and hold aside. Dredge the short ribs in flour seasoned with salt and pepper. Brown the ribs on all sides in the vegetable pan. Place the vegetables in the bottom of a roasting pan.

Place the browned short ribs with the bone down on top of the vegetables. Add salt and pepper, Port wine, chicken broth and garlic cloves. Use enough liquid to almost cover the meat, but do not cover completely.

Place plastic wrap and then tin foil on top to create a good seal. Braise in a preheated oven at 250 degrees for 8 hours. Remove and let stand for 30 minutes.

DEMI-GLACE: Strain cooking liquid into a sauce pot and bring to a boil. Reduce heat to a simmer until the right consistency is achieved. Strain through a fine mesh strainer twice. Adjust seasonings and serve with short ribs.

FINISHING: Serve over home-style mashed potatoes and grilled asparagus. Sauce should be ladled generously over the ribs.

SamVera

In a grand, 19th-century mansion, SamVera restaurant creates fine Italian cuisine, with an emphasis on fresh ingredients and elegant presentation.

Patrons dine at a leisurely pace, in surroundings that encourage relaxation. The floors of the bar and the two-story terrace gleam with granite and marble. Route 520 in Marlboro has retained some of its pastoral charm, despite increasing development, so it is pleasant to dine on the terrace.

The cocktail room features a mahogany bar topped with black granite, and matching café tables. French doors open to the main dining room, in a cream, tan and rose color scheme.

A banquet room upstairs can accommodate up to 75 guests.

SamVera is open Tuesdays through Thursdays from noon to 10 p.m. Fridays 4 p.m. to 11 p.m. Sundays from 1 p.m. to 9 p.m.

476 Route 520
Marlboro, NJ 07746
(732) 834-9889
www.samvera.com

Blackened Swordfish

Swordfish Seasoned with Cayenne Pepper Over SamVera Famous Mashed Potatoes for One

INGREDIENTS

8-ounce swordfish steak

2 soup spoons paprika

1 soup spoon crushed red pepper flakes

1 teaspoon black pepper

½ cup breadcrumbs

½ teaspoon cumin

¼ teaspoon cayenne pepper

½ stick butter

½ cup white wine

½ cup fish stock

2 tablespoons balsamic vinegar

GARNISHES: bell and sweet red peppers, eggplant, tomato, lettuce, cherry tomato, endive leaves and a fresh sprig of basil.

SWORDFISH: Mix paprika, red, black and cayenne pepper, breadcrumbs in a plate. Spread the mix thinly and then coat both sides of the fish.

Preheat cast iron skillet on high with ½ stick of butter. Cook each side of the fish for three minutes. Add ½ cup of white wine, ½ cup of fish stock and 2 tablespoons of balsamic vinegar. Cook over medium heat until sauce is reduced by half and fish is tender and cooked in the center.

FINISHING: Place fish over mashed potatoes or parsnips, if desired, and garnish with slices of bell and sweet peppers, eggplant, endive leaves, basil and topped with a tomato cut into a rose.

Sawa Hibachi Steakhouse and Sushi Bar

Anchored along the busy Eatontown intersection of Routes 35 and 36, Sawa Hibachi Steakhouse and Sushi Bar does a brisk business at lunch, as well as dinner.

Professionals on lunch break, moms with babies, and young couples can all be found downing sushi and enjoying the sizzle of the hibachi.

Bare wooden tables complement the angled wooden ceilings of the pagoda-like building. Children gravitate toward a large fish tank near the entrance, containing enormous fish, each at least a foot long.

A private room is available for up to 24 people.

Lunch is served from 11:30 a.m. to 2:30 p.m. Mondays through Fridays, and 1:30 to 3:30 p.m. Sundays. Dinner is served from 4:30 to 10:30 p.m. Mondays through Thursdays; 4:30 to 11 p.m. Fridays, 3 to 11 p.m. Saturdays and 3:30 to 10:30 p.m. Sundays.

42 Route 36,
Eatontown, NJ 07724
(732) 544-8885
www.sawasteakhouse.com

Sawa Pepper Tuna

Peppered Tuna with Ponzu Sauce for One

INGREDIENTS

TUNA

sushi-grade tuna steak, cut to 7 inches by 3 inches by 0.8 inches

black pepper, finely ground

PONZU SAUCE

1 cup soy sauce

¾ cup lemon juice

¼ cup rice wine vinegar

1 teaspoon fresh ginger juice

½ cup dried bonito flakes

1 teaspoon sake (optional)

1 teaspoon mirin (Japanese cooking wine, optional)

PONZU SAUCE: Whisk together the sauce ingredients in a suitably sized bowl. Set aside.

TUNA: Cover entire tuna steak with fine ground black pepper. Lightly grill outside of tuna. Naturally cool the grilled tuna, or place in refrigerator for about 1 hour.

FINISHING: Cut the tuna steak into thin slices. Serve with ponzu sauce.

2 Senza

Red Bank is most glamorous at the Galleria, a collection of boutiques and restaurants in a carefully restored factory on Bridge Avenue.

The Italian restaurant 2 Senza uses the artistry of chef Bernardo Veliz and the environment—exposed beams and brick walls, tall windows and high ceilings—to fine advantage. 2 Senza has an open kitchen, and the hustle and bustle in that stainless-steel showcase indeed recalls a factory at work.

But diners will find that the pace is leisurely and that the food, served on wooden tables as Italian pop music fills the air, is authentically European.

2 Senza is closed Mondays. Lunch is served from 11:30 a.m. to 2:30 p.m. Tuesdays through Fridays. Dinner hours begin at 5 p.m. Tuesdays through Sundays. Events can be held on site, including weddings, bar and bat mitzvahs, showers and corporate functions.

2 Bridge Ave.
Red Bank, NJ 07701
(732) 758-0999
www.2senza.com

Risotto con Astice

Risotto with Lobster for Four

INGREDIENTS

LOBSTER

3 lobsters, 1½ pounds each

2 carrots, diced

2 chopped celery stalks

1 leek

2 tablespoons tomato paste

2 cups white wine

¼ cup olive oil

RISOTTO

1 pound arborio rice

2 tablespoons butter

3 shallots, finely chopped

1½ to 2 cups hot lobster stock (to be made from lobster dish)

1 cup white wine

2 sprigs fresh tarragon, leaves chopped

salt to taste

LOBSTER AND STOCK: Place lobsters in a large stock pot, cover with water and bring to boil. At first boil, remove lobsters from the pot with tongs. Reserve liquid for stock. Be sure not to overcook the lobsters.

Separate each lobster tail from the body with a gentle twist and remove the claws. Gently remove the lobster meat from the tail and carefully crack the claws, saving the meat for the finished dish. Save the body and shells.

In the stock pot heat ¼ cup olive oil. Saute carrots, celery and leeks and deglaze with 2 cups of white wine. Add 2 tablespoons of tomato paste and reduce for 2 – 3 minutes. Add reserved lobster broth to the pot and bring to a boil for 5 minutes. Skim, reduce heat and simmer approximately 20 minutes. Strain stock and keep warm for use with rice.

RISOTTO: In large pan, sauté rice in butter and shallots. When shallots are soft and rice absorbs the butter, add white wine and stir. When rice absorbs the wine, slowly add the 1½ to 2 cups of hot lobster stock, stirring constantly. When rice is about 80 percent cooked, add the lobster medallions and claws, season with salt and pepper. Serve al dente.

The Little Kraut

For more than 30 years, the restaurant has been a Red Bank landmark on Oakland Street, just across from the train station. The Little Kraut's cottage exterior adds a quaint touch to the neighborhood. Patio seating makes for comfortable trainspotting.

Inside, purple lace curtains brighten the dark wood interior. Antlers hang on the wall, as do wooden shoes, and a pendulum clock keeps a steady vigil.

Dieter Bornemann, a master chef from Gottinger, Germany, remains at the helm. He comes from a long line of acclaimed pastry makers in Germany. His menu highlights his native German cuisine, but also other Continental specialties, including frogs' legs, prepared in myriad ways.

Lunch is available only to private parties.

The Little Kraut is closed Mondays. Dinner hours are 5 to 10 p.m. Tuesdays through Thursdays, 5 to 11 p.m. Fridays and Saturdays, and 3 to 9 p.m. Sundays.

115 Oakland St.
Red Bank, NJ 07701
(732) 842-4830
www.littlekraut.com

Venison Roulade

Served with Homemade Red Cabbage and Spaetzl and Dumpling for One

INGREDIENTS

(2) 4-ounce medallions of venison

¼ cup venison broth (can be substituted with beef or chicken stock, but venison broth is best)

2 Granny Smith apples, peeled and cored, sliced ¼-inch thick

⅓ cup Calvados liqueur

1 tablespoon butter

½ onion, diced

2 teaspoons lingonberries, in their own juices

3 slices white bread with crust removed

1 cup milk

1 tablespoon olive oil

salt and pepper to taste

paprika to taste

STUFFING: Marinate apples in Calvados overnight. In a small sauté pan, melt butter over medium heat and add onions. Sauté until golden brown, and then cool. In a large sauté pan, melt 1 tablespoon butter over medium-high heat. Add marinated apples and lingonberries. Sauté until apples are caramelized as a deep, golden brown. Set aside.

Soak bread in milk until tender then gently squeeze out excess milk. Set aside.

VENISON: Preheat oven to 400 degrees. Oil the medallions and season with salt, pepper and paprika, to taste. Heat a medium cast iron sauté pan over high heat. As it begins to smoke, add medallions. Sear for 1 minute on each side. Remove from heat. Equally divide the stuffing among the medallions, spread evenly and roll. Lightly coat the bottom of the cast iron pan with oil. Placing the open end on the bottom, return the roulades to the pan. Place in oven and braise for 3 minutes to sear the roulades closed.

FINISHING: Remove pan from oven. Place the roulades on a warm plate and keep dish warm. Return pan to stove over medium heat. Deglaze with venison broth, stirring while scraping the bottom of the pan to lessen all the juices, until liquid has been reduced to about 1 tablespoon. Add remaining apple-lingonberries mixture and mix well. Season with salt and pepper to taste. Serve over roulades.

Clarks Bar & Grill

Unparalleled views of the Manasquan River can be had at Clarks Bar & Grill.

The restaurant stands at the river's edge and overlooks a marina, so diners can enjoy watching the boats come and go. Clark's is accented with oceanic tones, such as the blue tiles bordering the kitchen or the sea-green lamps that hang over the bare-wood tables.

Seafood and Continental dishes are prominent on the menu.

From Labor Day until Memorial Day, the restaurant is closed Mondays and Tuesdays. Clark's serves lunch from 11:30 a.m. to 5 p.m. and dinner from 5 to 10 p.m., Wednesdays through Sundays. Happy hours are 4 to 6 p.m. Wednesdays through Fridays.

A tiki bar on the back patio is open daily, weather permitting. Parties, from casual get-togethers at the tiki bar to small weddings, can be booked for 15 to 75 guests.

847 Arnold Ave.
Point Pleasant, NJ 08742
(732) 899-1111
www.clarksbarandgrill.com

Seared Red Snapper

Seared Red Snapper with Avocado-Crab Mashed Potatoes for Two

INGREDIENTS

SAUCE

3 tablespoons virgin olive oil

8 ounces diced tomatoes

8 leaves fresh basil

10 slices fresh garlic

4 ounces white wine

2 ounces fish stock

1 fresh lemon, squeezed for juice

4 ounces butter

salt and pepper to taste

POTATOES & SNAPPER

2 large potatoes, preferably Idaho, boiled until soft

6 ounces milk

4 ounces butter

10 to 12 pieces lump crab meat

ripe avocado

2 8-ounce red snapper filets

salt and pepper to taste

SAUCE: In sauce pan, heat olive oil, add garlic slices and diced tomatoes. Stir constantly until hot and sizzling. Add wine, fish stock and fresh basil with ½ of lemon juice. Bring to a boil over medium-high heat. Boil 1 to 2 minutes to reduce, then add butter, salt and pepper. Stir until butter is melted.

POTATOES: Mash potatoes in mixer with milk and butter. When soft, add sliced avocado, mix until smooth. Add crab meat, salt and pepper. Mix until smooth and creamy.

SNAPPER: Preheat oven to 350 degrees. Score the skin on the snapper filets, then season with salt and pepper. Melt butter in a hot sauté pan, add filets, searing both sides until brown. Place in oven for 5 minutes.

FINISHING: Place mashed potatoes in the middle of the plate, lay the snapper on an angle on the potatoes, drizzle the sauce around the fish and finish with fresh basil. Serve with lemon wedge.

Europa South

To get to Europa South from downtown Point Pleasant Beach, just follow your nose.

A fragrant stream of garlic, brandy, peppers and seafood seems to emanate from this Portuguese/Spanish restaurant, a landmark on Arnold Avenue.

Inside, Europa South is warm and inviting, with dark wood and stained-glass accents. Red leather chairs at the dining tables suggest a comfortable evening. In the front room, a cozy bar is set against a brick wall.

The menu is traditional, specializing in seafood. Four kinds of soup are available daily, including gazpacho.

Europa South offers catering and the restaurant can accommodate banquets for up to 150 people.

The entertainer Alfredo Cunha performs Fridays and Saturdays.

Lunch is served Tuesdays through Saturdays, from 11:30 a.m. to 3 p.m. Dinner hours are 4 to 10 p.m. Tuesdays through Thursdays; 4 to 11 p.m. Fridays and Saturdays; and 12 p.m. to 9 p.m. Sundays.

521 Arnold Ave. and Route 35 South
Point Pleasant Beach, NJ 08742
(732) 295-1500
www.europasouth.com

Portuguese Cod

Fresh Cod Fish, Portuguese Style for One

INGREDIENTS

10-ounce filet of fresh cod, cut into 3 or 4 pieces (any fish can be substituted)

4 clams and 4 ounces clam juice

6 to 8 shrimp

1 tablespoon fresh garlic

2 ounces shallots

3 bay leaves

1 ounce olive oil

several pieces of cilantro

salt, pepper and flour

4 ounces heavy cream

1 tablespoon tomato sauce

2 ounces white wine

2 tablespoons Hollandaise sauce

FISH: Prepare the filet by sprinkling salt and pepper over it, then a thin coat of flour on both sides. Preheat oven to 400 degrees.

Place olive oil in pot and heat on medium high flame. Add garlic, shallots and let sizzle to a golden color.

Place the filet in the pot and add the white wine. Wait 20 seconds and add the clam juice. Allow to simmer for about a minute. Add clams and shrimp around the filet. Add heavy cream and tomato sauce to pot, shake or use a spoon to blend.

Place Hollandaise sauce on top of fish along with bay leaves and a few pieces of cilantro.

Place the pot in the preheated oven and allow to cook for 10 to 12 minutes. Add a few additional pieces of cilantro if desired.

FINISHING: The fish is best served with saffron rice.

Forte

Mediterranean cuisine goes beyond Italian to cover the entire sunny region, including dishes from Turkey and Greece.

John Ucal, a native of Turkey, highlights the food of his homeland at Forte, a Mediterranean restaurant in Point Pleasant. So the menu of his restaurant features grape leaves and eggplant dishes as well as seafood and pasta.

A cathedral ceiling, skylights and a sunburst window make the main dining room an airy space. Ornate rugs hang on the walls that lead to the restaurant's upstairs dining area, which has a fireplace and can be used for banquets and private parties.

Guests can be entertained by belly dancers on certain nights.

Happy hours in the bar are 5 to 7 p.m. Mondays through Fridays.

Lunch is served from 11:30 a.m. to 2:30 p.m. Mondays through Fridays. Dinner is served daily from 3:30 to about 10 p.m.

2154 Bridge Ave.
Point Pleasant, NJ 08742
(732) 899-5600
www.forteuniquecuisines.com

Shrimp Pernod

Shrimp served with Creamy Sweet Red Roasted Pepper Sauce for Two

....

INGREDIENTS

12 large shrimp

1 cup olive oil

2 whole red roasted sweet peppers

1 bag fresh spinach

4 cloves chopped garlic

1 stick butter

2 cups heavy cream

2 ounces Pernod liquor

¼ box pasta of your choice

salt and pepper to taste

SHRIMP: Heat oil in sauté pan and add shrimp when oil is hot. Cook evenly on both sides. Add Pernod liquor and cook down. Add heavy cream and butter.

PASTA: Remove shrimp from pan. Add sliced red roasted peppers, garlic and cooked pasta.

FINISHING: Remove pasta from pan and place on plate. Add spinach to pan and sauté. Remove spinach and place next to pasta.

Place shrimp over pasta and add remaining sauce to plate.

George's Grill

Musical instruments "float" in a verdant grove. Tiny purple lights twinkle. Purple, in fact, is the reigning hue throughout George's Grill, a sight for sore eyes off commercial Route 88.

It's all very "Midsummer Night's Dream," and, actually, the design scheme is based on a dream had by the Brazilian-born owner and chef, George Edward Kretzu. Kretzu has a fanciful sensibility—he bordered the ceiling of the ladies' room with lace from a bra—and that carries over to his menu. George's Grill serves Continental/Italian dishes with elements of South American cuisine. He offers diners his signature Double-Cut Slow-Roast Pork in four distinct styles.

George's Grill is open seven days a week, from 6 a.m. to 11 p.m., serving breakfast, lunch and dinner. The restaurant also delivers and does off-premises catering.

2030 Route 88
Brick, NJ 08724
(732) 206-0603

Green Mist Chicken

Chicken with a Light Pesto Basil Sauce for One

INGREDIENTS

(1) 8-ounce chicken breast

8 asparagus pencils

6 artichoke heart halves

2 ounces thin sliced garlic

3 ounces peas

3 ounces sliced Vidalia onion

3 ounces pesto basil sauce

3 ounces sliced fresh tomato

4 ounces penne pasta, cooked

2 ounces extra-virgin olive oil

3 ounces Parmigiano-Reggiano cheese, grated

CHICKEN: Grill chicken, slice thinly and set aside.

PASTA: In a sauté pan, add 2 ounces of olive oil, onions and garlic. Sauté until tender.

Add asparagus, artichokes, peas and pesto to sautéed garlic and onion. Add the sliced tomato and pasta. Toss all in sauté pan for 3 – 5 minutes.

FINISHING: Serve on platter, top with grilled chicken and grated cheese.

Il Giardino Sul Mare

A branch of the Forked River runs directly behind Il Giardino Sul Mare, providing a soothing backdrop to the fine Italian restaurant.

Il Giardino is an oasis in the Wharfside Plaza shopping center. The river can be seen from most areas of the restaurant. Three rooms on the main level, plus a deck adjacent to the river, accommodate individual parties, while separate rooms can be booked for parties and banquets for 25 to 100 guests.

The dark-wood tables and chairs are tastefully appointed with white tablecloths. Art work of Italy hangs on the walls.

Il Giardino is a sister restaurant to Villa Vittoria in Brick and is owned by the same group of former waiters—Nelson and Olmedo Monroy, Jacinto and Dago Segura, and Ciro Bojaca.

The restaurant serves lunch and dinner, with early-bird specials weekdays from 4 to 5:35 p.m. and five-course specials on Thursday evenings.

Hours are Mondays through Fridays, 11:30 a.m. to 9 p.m.; Saturdays, 1 to 10 p.m.; and Sundays, 1 to 9 p.m. A pianist performs on Wednesdays.

2 Hollywood Blvd.
Forked River, NJ 08731
(609) 971-7699
www.ilgiardinorestaurant.com

Vitello a Granchio Mamma Mia

Veal Scallopine in a Madeira Wine Reduction for One

INGREDIENTS

4 ounces veal scallopine

flour

olive oil

½ teaspoon chopped garlic

2 teaspoons Madeira wine

6 ounces demi-glace sauce

1 ounce marinara sauce

mushrooms: 1 each portobello, shiitake and button

1 ounce crab meat

salt, pepper and basil

VEAL & SAUCE: Thinly pound 4 ounces of veal scallopine, then coat with flour, using fancy flour if available.

On a medium burner, pan-fry with olive oil. Add chopped garlic and sauté until golden brown.

Add Madeira wine, demi-glace and marinara sauce to the pan and reduce.

Add mushrooms and continue to reduce until mushrooms are tender. Finally add the crabmeat and turn burner off.

FINISHING: Add salt, pepper and basil to complement the flavor.

La Strada Ristorante

As Route 88 winds westward through Brick, there stands La Strada, always ready for a hungry customer.

With three menus—lunch, early dinner and regular dinner—it seems like La Strada is always open. The staples of Italian-American cuisine, with a Portuguese accent, from cacciatore to cavatelli, comprise the bulk of each menu. Burgundy tablecloths and exposed brick walls set a warm tone in this popular Italian restaurant, which also offers catering and private parties.

Hours are 11:30 a.m. to 10 p.m. Mondays through Fridays; 3 to 10 p.m. Saturdays, and 2 to 9 p.m. Sundays.

1643 Route 88 West
Brick, NJ 08724
(732) 458-5228
www.lastradaonline.net

Veal La Strada

Veal Scallopine Sauteed in Portwine Sauce Topped with Prosciutto, Fried Eggplant and Mozzarella for Two

INGREDIENTS

8 pieces veal scallopine (1 pound total)

1 teaspoon sea salt

1 teaspoon black pepper

2 large eggs, lightly beaten

1 large eggplant, sliced thin

3 slices prosciutto

½ cup Port

½ cup beef stock

½ cup chicken stock

8 pieces sliced fresh mozzarella

4 tablespoons pure olive oil

VEAL: Heat 2 tablespoons oil in oven-proof skillet. Brush the veal scallopine lightly with oil and season them with salt and pepper. Sear the veal in the skillet over high heat, turning occasionally until brown, about 3 to 4 minutes.

Remove the oil. Pour the Port wine over the veal and cook for 2 minutes. Add the beef and chicken stock and continue cooking for another 6 to 8 minutes.

Preheat the oven to 400 degrees.

EGGPLANT: Fry the eggplant in 2 tablespoons of olive oil in a second skillet. Dip the eggplant in eggs and cook for about 3 to 4 minutes on each side.

FINISHING: Place the fried eggplant and prosciutto, followed by the mozzarella, on top of the veal scallopine. Place the skillet into the oven and cook for 8 to 10 minutes, or until the cheese melts.

Mario's South Italian Seafood Grill & Market

Mario's South has its own seafood market next door to the restaurant, so it's no surprise that this traditional Italian-American restaurant specializes in fresh-from-the-sea fare.

The restaurant is located in a strip mall off busy Hooper Avenue. Mario's softens the environment with shaded votive candles on every table and a mural of flowers and vines on the wall.

Banquet service can accommodate up to 120 guests. Mario's also can provide off-premises catering. Hours are 3 to 9 p.m. Tuesdays through Thursdays; 3 to 10 p.m. Fridays and Saturdays; and 1 to 9 p.m. Sundays. The restaurant is closed on Mondays, except during the summer.

1747 Hooper Ave.
Toms River, NJ 08753
(732) 255-6333
www.mariossouth.com

Red Snapper Brodetta

Snapper Poached in a White Wine Sauce with Clams and Mussels for One

INGREDIENTS

10-ounce filet of red snapper with skin removed

3 littleneck clams

3 mussels

½ boiled potato chopped into ½-inch pieces

6 black olives

6 capers

½ white onion, diced

fresh basil leaves, parsley and oregano

crushed red hot pepper

2 ounces blended oil

1 teaspoon butter

2 cloves diced garlic

4 ounces chicken stock

4 ounces white wine

SNAPPER: Heat oil in sauté pan. Add snapper, clams and mussels. Sauté for 1 minute. Add garlic, chicken stock, white wine, 4 leaves of basil, a large pinch of chopped parsley, a large pinch of oregano, potato, olives, capers, onion and butter. Add crushed red pepper to taste.

Cover pot. Cook over low flame for 6 to 8 minutes or until fish is tender to the touch.

FINISHING: Serve on a platter or over a bed of angel hair pasta or with rice and vegetables.

Oil House Café

Oil House Café is a charming little eatery in the Stella Towne Center mall on Route 166, just a few miles before the highway turns into Main Street, Toms River.

Strings of lights, potted trees and bistro tables create a patio effect on the sidewalk outside the restaurant. Inside, black metal tables and chairs are dressed up with blue and white linens. Plants and candles add cheer and coziness.

The walls are decorated with photographs of European landmarks, which hints at the menu. Oil House Café specializes in steaks and seafood, and the fare ranges from scallops Alfredo to fish and chips to cheese and spinach Filos. The restaurant features "Middle Eastern Night" on the last Friday of the month.

Oil House Café is closed Mondays.

From Tuesdays through Thursdays, an early dinner is served from 3 p.m. to closing. Early dinner is served from 3 to 5 p.m. Fridays through Sundays.

Regular dinner hours begin at 5 p.m. Tuesdays through Saturdays; Sundays 2 p.m. to 7 p.m.

Catering is available, with an emphasis on luncheons, business gatherings and personal parties.

1218 Route 166
Toms River, NJ 08753
(732) 244-4060
www.oilhousecafe.com

Schnitzel a la Holstein

Veal Scallopine Topped with Fried Egg and Anchovies for Two

INGREDIENTS

BREADING

2 cups flour

2 eggs

1 cup milk

2 cups bread crumbs

VEAL

(4) 4-ounce veal cutlets (scallopine)

Salt and pepper to taste

½ cup shallots, finely chopped

4 ounces lemon juice

1 egg

olive oil or butter

anchovies

VEAL: Lightly flatten each piece of veal with a mallet. Do not pound too hard, or the veal may tear.

Mix the salt, pepper, shallots and lemon juice in a large bowl and marinate the veal in the mixture for 2 to 4 hours before cooking.

BREADING: Combine the breading ingredients in another large bowl. Pass the marinated veal through the breading. Heat about ¼ inch of butter or similar amount of olive oil in large sauté pan. Place the cutlets in the pan, turn and cook until golden brown on both sides. Remove from pan onto plate.

FINISHING: Add a small amount of oil to the hot pan. Fry 1 egg, place it on top of the veal and surround with anchovies.

Pilot House

From the outside, Pilot House appears as if it is a stubby lighthouse hugging the Metedeconk River.

Inside, the restaurant looks like a nautical pub. Flags and kayaks hang from the high ceiling. The bar is front-and-center when you come in, with a neon light above it that proclaims "Pilot House." Locals gather for a drink on the weekdays, and it becomes a happening scene on the weekends, especially in the summer. Live music is offered Thursdays and Fridays, year 'round.

But dining is the top priority for Michael Tufariello, the owner. He's proud of the sushi bar, the Sunday brunch, the seafood and steaks.

Tables line a curved wall of windows, providing plenty of river view seating, with boats in the Forge Landing Marina providing a picturesque backdrop.

Dinner is served daily, beginning at 4 p.m. Sunday brunch is offered from 10:30 a.m. to 2 p.m.

799 Route 70, at Forge Landing Marina
Brick, NJ 08723
(732) 920-8900
www.pilothousenj.com

Herb-Crusted Salmon

Herb Crusted Salmon with Fresh Tomato and Kalamata Olive Compote for Four

INGREDIENTS

4 salmon filets

1 tablespoon chopped garlic

1 cup chopped plum tomatoes

½ cup Kalamata olives

¼ cup chopped fresh basil

¼ cup chopped fresh parsley

3 tablespoons extra-virgin olive oil

salt to taste

pinch of sugar

COMPOTE: Sauté garlic and plum tomatoes in 2 tablespoons of olive oil. Add the Kalamata olives, balsamic vinegar and sugar. Simmer about 5 minutes. Add half of the fresh herbs and season with salt. Set aside.

SALMON: Coat salmon with the other half of the fresh herbs. Heat a sauté pan, coat with olive oil and sear salmon on high heat for 1 minute. Turn fish and place in 300-degree oven for 10 minutes.

FINISHING: Serve over roasted garlic mashed potatoes. Top with the fresh tomato and Kalamata olive sauce.

Plantation Restaurant

Plantation, one of Long Beach Island's most acclaimed restaurants, evokes island style on a grand scale.

Chef Jeff Alberti takes inspiration from islands far from LBI, with a menu influenced by Caribbean and Latin cuisines. Beans and island fruits accent seafood and meat dishes. The cocktail list boasts a renowned mojito and a special Plantation Bloody Mary.

Louvered shutters and hanging baskets decorate the exterior of the building, in the heart of Harvey Cedars' small business district. Inside, the atmosphere is relaxed and elegant, with wicker chairs and fabric-shaded chandeliers. Tones of sand, brown and moss can be found on the furniture, on the walls and in table settings.

Plantation bustles all year long. A fireplace anchors one end of the dining room, hinting at convivial times in the off-season. It even offers separate vegetarian and gluten-free menus, to accommodate a variety of dietary needs.

Plantation is open seven days a week, serving lunch from 11:30 a.m. to 2:30 p.m. and light fare from 2:30 to 4 p.m. Summertime dinner hours are 4 to 10 p.m. Sundays through Thursdays, and 4 to 11 p.m. Fridays and Saturdays.

Off-season dinner hours are 4 to 10 p.m. daily.

7908 Long Beach Blvd.
Harvey Cedars, NJ 08008
(609) 494-8191
www.plantationrestaurant.com

Plantation Crab Cakes

Crab Cakes with Corn Salsa for Ten

INGREDIENTS

CRAB CAKES

2 cups real mayonnaise

3 eggs

4 pounds jumbo lump crab meat

3 tablespoons adobo sauce

¼ bunch cilantro, washed

½ lime, juice only

1 red pepper

1 poblano

½ bunch scallions

2 tablespoons Worcestershire sauce

4 tablespoons Dijon mustard

Sea salt, to taste

1 cup panko (Japanese) bread crumbs

6 cloves roasted garlic

½ cup semolina

CORN SALSA

8 cobs of corn in husk

1 red pepper

½ red onion

½ bunch scallions

½ bunch cilantro

2 ounces red wine vinegar

1 teaspoon cumin

3 teaspoons smoked paprika

2 limes, juice and zest only

8 peppadew peppers, diced small

salt to taste

4 tablespoons extra-virgin olive oil

CRAB CAKES: Puree in blender the roasted garlic with adobo sauce, lime juice, Dijon mustard and Worcestershire sauce and cilantro. Pour into mixing bowl.

Dice red pepper and poblano into small pieces. Chop scallions. Combine in bowl with garlic puree. Add eggs and mayonnaise.

Add panko, season with 1 teaspoon of salt to start.

Open crab meat and discard extra liquid. Gently fold crab into all other ingredients. Make each portion about 4 ounces. Dredge in semolina and fry in Teflon sauté pan.

Leftover crab cakes can be frozen for future dinners if wrapped tightly in plastic wrap.

CORN SALSA: Roast corn in husk, with some of the outer husk removed, and trim top and bottom before roasting. Dice red pepper and and onion. Sauté in very hot pan for 1 minute, then add vinegar, cumin and smoked paprika. Sauté one minute more or until liquid is reduced.

Remove from heat, add lime juice and zest. Strip roasted corn off cobs. Combine with scallions, cilantro, peppadew peppers and olive oil.

Makes 20 cakes.

Solo Bella

On Sundays, you eat what Mama puts in front of you. Solo Bella is a brick-oven bistro with a homespun sense of nostalgia. The weekly specials are designed to mimic what a typical Jersey-Italian family grew up with, right down to the surprise menu on Sundays.

The bistro is casual and contemporary. There's also a patio for outdoor seating. The menu features thin-crust, brick-oven pizza as well as Italian-American specialties and a shrimp cocktail with shrimp as long as your finger.

Solo Bella is located in a freestanding building that looks like a house, pale yellow with blue shutters. The cross street is Jackson Mills Road.

Solo Bella is about a mile from Six Flags Great Adventure, making it the perfect spot for a family dinner after a day on roller coasters and log flumes.

The restaurant serves lunch and dinner daily. Hours are 11 a.m. to 10 p.m. weekdays and 11 a.m. to 11 p.m. weekends.

426 Chandler Road
Jackson, NJ 08527
(732) 961-0951
www.solobella.com

Concetta's Famous Meatballs and Sauce

Macaroni and Meatballs for Ten

INGREDIENTS

SAUCE

4 boxes Pomi strained tomatoes

1 large onion

2 cloves peeled garlic

10 to 12 leaves fresh basil (chop in half)

salt and pepper to taste

¼ cup olive oil

6 links sweet Italian sausage

MEATBALLS

5 pounds ground sirloin beef

10 eggs

1½ cups breadcrumbs (preferably homemade)

1 cup blended oil

1 cup fresh grated Pecorino Romano cheese

8 to 10 cloves fresh garlic

bunch of Italian parsley

salt and pepper

MACARONI

2 pounds of your favorite macaroni

1 pound fresh whole milk ricotta cheese

grated Pecorino Romano cheese (preferably buy solid cheese and grate fresh)

SAUCE: In medium size sauce pot add olive oil and finely chop onion. Add six links of sweet Italian sausage, brown onion and sausage on medium flame. Take care not to burn the onions. Slice the garlic cloves in half and add to pot.

When garlic is brown, add tomatoes. Add salt and pepper to taste and cook approximately one hour on medium heat, stirring with a wooden spoon only. Add freshly chopped basil. Reduce flame to simmer with cover off and let simmer for 30 minutes, stirring with spoon.

MEATBALLS: In a large bowl or pot mix chopped meat, breadcrumbs and eggs. Finely chop garlic and parsley and add to meat mixture. Add the grated cheese, salt and pepper to taste.

Add a little water, if the mixture feels too dry, until it feels just right. Once mixed, put bowl on the counter top near the stove and get a small cup of cold water ready for dipping.

On a butcher block, start rolling the meatballs. Dip your hands in cold water so the meatballs do not stick to your hands. Roll the meatballs into an oval shape. Make sure each meatball is smooth without craters or holes. This batch makes 50 to 60 meatballs.

In a frying pan on medium flame, heat up one cup of oil (blended oil or pomace oil is best). Place meatballs in when the oil is hot. Fry on all sides to golden brown.

Put most of the fried meatballs into the sauce but leave some out for the last 10 minutes (the meatballs soak up a lot of sauce).

MACARONI: In a large stock pot, add a dash of salt to the water that will be used to boil the macaroni. Cook macaroni to the desired tenderness then strain well.

Place the meatballs and sausage in a large bowl on the table. Transfer the macaroni to the bowl, add a couple of scoops of sauce and a spoon of ricotta on top.

FINISHING: Serve with Italian bread, grated cheese and whole milk ricotta (optional).

Villa Vittoria

Villa Vittoria is a labor of love for its owners because they all were long-time waiters at the restaurant before they became its owners.

Nelson and Olmedo Monroy, Jacinto and Dago Segura, and Ciro Bojaca remain loyal to the sensibility of the restaurant's original owner, Giuseppe Salpietro.

Fine Italian cuisine, with an emphasis on traditional appetizers, pasta dishes, veal and seafood, remains the focus at the brick building on the corner of Old Hooper and Cedar Bridge avenues.

Decorative wine bottles and figurines line a shelf. Frosted mirrors and paintings and photos of Italian villas hang on the walls. The restaurant is cozy and elegant, with a color scheme of cream and forest green.

Live music adds to the atmosphere on Thursdays, with vocalists performing standards by Frank Sinatra and other like-minded artists.

Villa Vittoria serves lunch and dinner.

Hours are 11:30 a.m. to 9:30 p.m. Mondays through Fridays; 1 to 10 p.m. Saturdays; and 1 to 9:30 p.m. Sundays.

Villa Vittoria is a sister restaurant to Il Giardino Sul Mare in Forked River.

2700 Old Hooper Ave.
Brick, NJ 08724
(732) 920-1550
www.villavittoria.com

Zuppa di Pesce

Seafood in a White Wine Sauce for One

INGREDIENTS

SEAFOOD

(1) 3-ounce lobster tail

4 ounces scallops

2 medium shrimp

2 little neck clams

3 ounces calamari, sliced

3 New Zealand mussels

SAUCE

3 teaspoons extra-virgin olive oil

1 garlic clove, sliced

1 ounce white wine

salt and pepper

4 leaves fresh basil

8 ounces fresh plum tomatoes

12 ounces linguine

PASTA: Precook pasta before preparing the dish. Cook the linguine for 7 minutes in salted boiling water.

SEAFOOD AND SAUCE: Heat sauté pan very hot. Add 3 teaspoons of the olive oil, the sliced garlic and the seafood. Simmer for 1 minute. Add the white wine, the basil, the plum tomatoes, the salt and the pepper, to taste. Simmer for 3 or 4 minutes until lobster tail is firm.

FINISHING: Remove the precooked linguine and place on a plate. Add the seafood and finally pour the sauce over the seafood and the pasta.

Wine Suggestions

Red Wine

Red wines are produced in virtually all of the world's wine regions and range in color from dark pink to almost black. Recent studies have shown that drinking a glass of red wine a day may have certain health benefits.

White Wine

White wines range in color from virtually colorless to deep gold, with a taste of each wine as different as the places from which they come. White wines are served chilled just under 50 degrees.

Sparkling Wine

Only wines that come from the Champagne region in France can be properly called "Champagne." All others from around the world are referred to as sparkling wines. Traditionally, sparkling wine has been used as a wine for celebrations and special occasions.

The following table of wines is just a sample of the wine varietals that exist. For help with other pairings, please contact us at 732-223-3180.

Food and Wine Pairings

Wine Type	Characteristics	Pairs with...
CHARDONNAY	Apple pear flavors with a creamy texture	Roasted Chicken, Lobster
SAUVIGNON BLANC/ PINOT GRIGIO	Fruity, medium-bodied and crisp	Clams, Fish, Fragrant Salads
REISLING	Made in different styles, from dry to sweet, with pear and mineral flavors	Asian food, Mussels, Roast Pork
MERLOT	Floral nose and a soft taste, smooth	Chocolate, Cheeseburgers
PINOT NOIR	Cherry and berry flavors, with varying degrees of complexity	Turkey, Port Tenderloins, Lamb
CABERNET SAUVIGNON	Full-bodied, with flavors of black fruits	T-Bone, Strip or Sirloin Steaks, Stews
ZINFANDEL	Spice, pepper and hints of chocolate-Robust	Beef, Pasta, Red Tomato Sauce
PORT	Fortified wine, sweet	Aged Cheeses, Walnuts, Dark Chocolate
SPARKLING WINE	Ranging from bone-dry to sweet, flavors of brioche and Crème Brule	Caviar, Oysters, Scallops, Also as an Aperitif

Making Wine Selection More Palatable

With so many wines to choose from, sometimes the task of picking up a bottle to go with dinner or as a gift is a daunting idea. The choice is made easy at Spirit of '76 because not only is the selection phenomenal, but the friendly, knowledgeable staff is always on hand to assist.

One of the best ways to learn about wine is to taste for yourself. FREE SATURDAY Samplings offer the customer a chance to try before you buy, with topics changing every week. Stop in on Saturdays from 2-5 pm and see for yourself.

SPIRIT OF '76
WINES & LIQUORS

Produce

The Original Country Food Market...

The Delicious Orchards market is over 60,000 square feet, half of which is devoted to produce. An incomparable selection of fruits and vegetables are on display. You'll find fresh from the field produce as each season arrives, from the finest local corn, tomatoes and peaches in the summer, to autumn when the apple harvest is in and the aroma of cider fills the air. Delicious Orchards is a year-round destination for the freshest and finest produce.

Give it a little squeeze...

Delicious Orchards features fresh daily produce brought to you at the peak of flavor. Crisp asparagus, perfectly sweet strawberries and varieties of apples are available throughout the year. Exotic items like Bok Choy, Ginger Root, Oriental Mushrooms, Swiss Chard are all here. All year round there are well-stocked bins of oranges, tangerines and minneolas alongside grapefruit, lemons and stone fruits such as plums, peaches and nectarines. Each night all products are taken out of the bins and stored in a separate cold storage area. Every morning they are carefully inspected again, inferior products discarded and all bins re-stocked to ensure quality and freshness.

The Nose Knows...

Tantalizing aromas abound in the bakery. There are the smells of fresh melting butter, cinnamon and pies baking—brimming with apple, pumpkin, rhubarb and strawberry filling. There are over eighty different products being baked daily including sugar-free items. There are buns and biscuits... breads, cookies, donuts - offered only minutes from their cooking ovens. Each contributing to the remarkable atmosphere which is Delicious Orchard's alone.

There's More to the Story...

Choose from over 600 cheeses from around the globe: Domestics include Cabot Extra Sharp, Vermont Private Stock and Wisconsin Colby Longhorn. Imported selections include Brie, Camembert and Swiss to name just a few. Just as impressive is the gourmet meat showcase containing the finest filets, roasts and the freshest chicken. For customers on the go, take-out items from salads to entire dinner selections are prepared daily. A gourmet section offers hard-to-find food specialties that mean so much when planning a party or just to have on hand as special treats for the whole family.

It's Worth The Trip.

Visit Delicious Orchards today and experience a unique, one-of-a-kind food shopping experience. For latest updates on in-season products, recipes, specials and directions to our store log on to
deliciousorchardsnj.com

Delicious Orchards
THE COUNTRY FOOD MARKET

Route 34, Colts Neck

deliciousorchardsnj.com (732) 462-1989, (732) 542-0204 Hours: 10 am to 6pm Tues. thru Sun., closed Mon.

Placesettings

Fine dinnerware adds a touch of elegance to any gourmet meal; it enhances the appeal of the food and leave a memorable impression on your guests. But like fine food, delicate glassware, silverware and china need tender, loving care to keep it in its best shape. Here are a few tips:

Crystal

While the best lead crystal feels heavy in your hands, its weight belies its fragile nature. Gentle washing is needed to ensure the rims do not chip and the luster does not fade away. Experts recommend that you wash crystal by hand in warm water with a mild lemon dish detergent and about one-quarter cup ammonia, which is used to prevent spotting. Rinse in clean water and let air dry on a dish rack. An automatic dishwasher can be harsh on crystal and diminish its brilliance. Never place metal-accented crystal, such as glasses with a gold rim, in the dishwasher. If you find you need to use a dish washer, select the "fine china/crystal" setting and use only half of the recommended amount of detergent. Most detergents are abrasive and can leave minute scratches or pits. Ensure that the top rack is low enough to account for the height of the stemware and that the glassware does not bump against each other.

China

The best dinnerware is a family treasure, handed down through the generations. Masterpieces are hand-crafted with detailed painting and glazing. A hard glaze on the dinnerware does give a robust protection from forks and knives, but did you know china can be scratched by other china? Do not stack the dishes on top of each other, because the bottom of one plate can chip the top of another. Try placing a cloth pad or even a paper napkin between each plate to preserve their beauty.

Flatware

Silver flatware is tough enough for any dinner guest, but caution needs to be taken during cleaning time. The silver is easily scratched by abrasive cleaners. It is best to wash with a mild detergent in warm water. Do not let food stains remain on the flatware for very long. Salty or acidic foods can stain the silver, so try to at least rinse the flatware after the meal if you do not plan to wash it until the end of the night. Store silverware in a flannel-lined case to avoid tarnishing.

Tools of the Trade

Knives - One of the most essential tools of the kitchen, a well-crafted knife will pay for itself many times over. Just as there are many different wines for many different tastes, knives come in all shapes and sizes.

No kitchen should be without the following cutlery: 3-inch parer for small jobs; 8-inch carver; 8-inch chef's knife; 5-inch serrated utility knife; kitchen shears; and sharpening steel. Be sure to keep your cutlery sharp. The best way is to "steel" it prior to each use. A dull knife can be dangerous to a cook because more pressure must be used to make a deep cut.

Cookware - For the most versatile cookware, look for products that have a heavy bottom that are made for both the stovetop and oven. A stainless steel interior clad over copper and aluminum is best for durability and even heating. Other options include non-stick pots and pans for ease of cleaning, and cast iron cookware for searing.

Gadgets

No kitchen should be without a blender, mixer and a food processor. Look for blenders that offer a large glass container, a heavy base for stability and easily removable blades for cleaning. A mixer is an essential labor saver for those repetitive chores, such as blending ingredients into a sauce or kneading dough. A hand blender is useful for quick chores. A food processor can easily chop vegetables and even meat into small chunks to save you time and effort.

The well-stocked kitchen

For the everyday cook in you, we have measuring tools, spatulas, graters and timers. And for your inner chef, we offer cooking torches, decorating cutlery and pastry tools. Everything you want and need to stock your kitchen at a great price.

Boscov's

where the buys are

boscovs.com 732-578-9115 Monmouth Mall, Rt 35, Eatontown
732-505-0770 Ocean County Mall, Hooper Ave, Toms River

Shore Gourmet Restaurant Locations

1 Nicholas
160 Route 35 South
Middletown

2 Ashes Cigar Club
33 Broad St.
Red Bank

3 Avon Pavilion
600 Ocean Ave.
Avon

4 Cafe Colore
3333 Route 9 North
Freehold

5 Cask 591
591 Broadway
Long Branch

6 Christie's Italian Seafood Grill
2420 Route 9 South
Howell

7 Copper Canyon
51 First Ave.
Atlantic Highlands

8 Crown Palace
1285 Route 35
Middletown

9 David Burke Fromagerie
26 Ridge Road
Rumson

10 Doris & Ed's
348 Shore Dr.
Highlands

11 Drew's Bayshore Bistro
58 Broad St.
Keyport

12 Due Amici
420 Higgins Ave.
Brielle

13 Mahogany Grille
142 Main St.
Manasquan

14 Market in the Middle
516 Cookman Ave.
Asbury Park

15 Matisse
1300 Ocean Ave.
Belmar

16 McLoone's Riverside
816 Ocean Ave.
Sea Bright

17 Mister C's Beach Bistro
Ocean Ave. and Allen Ave.
Allenhurst

18 Ocean Place Resort & Spa
1 Ocean Blvd.
Long Branch

19 Palumbo's
Asbury Ave. & Green Grove Rd.
Tinton Falls

20 Pino's
448 Route 9 North
Marlboro

21 Raven & the Peach
740 River Road
Fair Haven

22 Rooney's Oceanfront Restaurant
100 Ocean Ave.
Long Branch

23 Sallee Tee's
33 West St.
Monmouth Beach

24 Salt Creek Grille
4 Bingham Ave.
Rumson

25 SamVera
476 Route 520
Marlboro

26 Sawa Hibachi Steakhouse
42 Route 36
Eatontown

27 2 Senza
2 Bridge Ave.
Red Bank

28 The Little Kraut
115 Oakland St.
Red Bank

29 Clarks Bar & Grill
847 Arnold Ave.
Point Pleasant

30 Europa South
521 Arnold Ave.
Point Pleasant Beach

31 Forte
2154 Bridge Ave.
Point Pleasant

32 George's Grill
2030 Route 88
Brick

33 Il Giardino Sul Mare
2 Hollywood Blvd.
Forked River

34 La Strada Ristorante
1643 Route 88 West
Brick

35 Mario's South
1747 Hooper Ave.
Toms River

36 Oil House Cafe
12188 Route 166
Toms River

37 Pilot House
799 Route 70
Brick

38 Plantation Restaurant
7908 Long Beach Blvd.
Harvey Cedars

39 Solo Bella
426 Chandler Road
Jackson

40 Villa Vittoria
2700 Old Hooper Ave.
Brick

Index